SON OF MONSTER KIDDING

BY MICHAEL LEGGE

SON OF MONSTER KIDDING

Other books by Michael Legge

Dr. Dreck B-Movie Museum

Monster Kidding

Lurking in the Late Night

Escape from the Domain

Reddy Boys Mysteries

Deader than Dead

The Deserted Drive-In

Chiller Killer

PREFACE

Ahhh...that age of wonderment and discovery. That amazing moment when you found out you were a Monster Kid, even though you wouldn't hear that term for decades to come. That happened to me at the age of 6. It was a Sunday afternoon in New Jersey and I was sitting on the floor of my room with G.I. Joe, Major Matt Mason and Captain Action, probably engaged in an all out battle. Playing on the floor because the comics section of the Sunday paper, or the "funnies" as we called them, were still spread out on my bed. A blob of Silly Putty on the paper, drying up because I didn't put it back into its plastic egg. It was at that moment that my father called me into the living room. He pointed at the television and said "I bet you never saw anything like this before," and he was right. There I stood transfixed watching "The Creature From the Black Lagoon" swimming underneath Julie Adams. For the next hour I didn't move from in front of the TV. It was at that moment that my young life changed forever...heck...my whole life changed forever!

Before this, the TV Guide was just a magazine that my parents used to see what was upcoming that week on television and for my mother to do the puzzle. That too changed as it became an invaluable tool in my ever growing desire to see every horror, sci-fi and fantasy movie I could. I would pore over that little tome from cover to cover looking for the "melodramas" which is how the horror movies were listed, or anything with a title that sounded remotely like something I would be interested in seeing. I was often fooled by movies with titles like "The Fiend Who Walked The West." This was all great, but it still didn't quell my growing, voracious appetite for all things horror, which I know worried my parents at times. I was totally obsessed. Poor Superman, Batman, Spider-Man and the Fantastic Four. They were all in the forefront of my life, only to now take a back seat. I was unaware that just a mere few weeks later, another life altering event would happen. The discovery of something that would make my comic books and TV Guide pale in comparison.

Every week I would accompany my father to the little corner store or the "sweet shop" as we called it, to get our weekend half gallon of Hershey's ice cream and a comic book. The owners were not so keen on returning their stock of comic books or magazines and it was not unusual for them to have six months worth of magazines and comics on hand. When we entered the store, I made my way to the metal, spinning comic rack and spun it around a few turns. For the first time, it didn't seem to hold much interest for me. Next to the rack was a haphazardly built wooden shelf with some magazines and the daily newspapers sitting atop it. Then something caught my eye. It was a magazine half covered by a newspaper. It was an eye, set against a blue-tan-greenish face. I pulled it out and was now confronted with the evil visage of "Mr. Hyde." Famous Monsters? My eyes bugged and I could hardly contain myself. But, 50¢? Let's see...12, 24, 36, 48...wow. It was the equivalent of 4 comic books! Would my dad go for that? I begged, groveled, said that I wouldn't ask for anything ever again. I don't know if it was the pleading look in my eyes, the fact that it would preoccupy me for the afternoon, or that it was a magazine and a step above comic books, but my father agreed. And he was right on the last two counts. It not only preoccupied me for the afternoon, but for several weeks, and I was getting an education. Driving home I thumbed through my treasure just to look at the pictures, but when I got home, I laid on my bed and started to read, I learned names like Boris Karloff, Bela Lugosi, and Lon Chaney Jr. In the future fright films section I learned about TV shows like "The Munsters," "The Addams Family," "Lost in Space." I learned about upcoming films like "Bride of the Moon," "King Kong Meets Frankenstein," "Jayne Mansfield Meets Frankenstein," "Hercules Meets Frankenstein," and "Planet of the Apes."

With each issue I was able to acquire, my horror education grew by leaps and bounds. In the late 60's, early 70's, I was finally able to see many of the films I had only read about in those pages, as shows like "Creature Feature" and "Chiller

Theatre" debuted and aired the Universal classics, the AIP classics and some that were not so classic. But I didn't care. I took them all in and loved every minute of it.

As I grew into a teen, my fixation started to wane, as my fixation on girls started to replace it. I never lost my love of it, but my focus was elsewhere as the run of Famous Monsters ended and life started to grow serious.

Then, yet another life altering event happened. Filmfax and Fangoria started to run a series of articles on Horror Hosts. I of course had heard of Zacherley and The Creep who started to host WNEW's Creature Feature in the 70's, but I knew very little about many of the other hosts around the country. Within those articles I found two hosts that really grabbed my attention...Ghoulardi and the original Svengoolie. At this point I had the internet at my disposal, so I started to search for any information about them and came across Count Gore's Horror Host group. It was there that I met many of the same friends I have today (including the author of this book) and people who had been hosts for a few years or were just starting out. It was then that I had decided to become a host myself, and Halloween Jack was born. I took the show to Cablevision and was given a Friday night time slot and was seen in 72 cities up and down the New Jersey coast. It was an exciting time, to share my love of horror and sci-fi, to share the movies I grew up with and to work with my fellow Horror Hosts in The Horror Host Underground.

It was in 2010 that I was able to take it a step further when I started working with The Monster Channel and created various other streaming channels on my own. At first the goal was to bring as many of these films that meant so much to me, to people who remembered them, or might not have seen them before. But now it has taken on a whole new meaning. It's become more about recreating these experiences for people to remember, or to create new memories. It's about that feeling of excitement that I and so many other Monster Kids felt when they first discovered all these films on television, in the theaters, at the drive-ins or in the pages of Famous Monsters. That is why I designed the channel to recreate a station that you may have watched as a child in the 60's, 70's or 80's, full of retro programming, horror, sci-fi, fantasy, mystery and even cartoons and kung fu, along with commercials and trailers and you can watch it all at www.themonsterchannel.com.   It's the ultimate Monster Kid experience, just like the book you are now holding in your hands. We want you to relive all that fun, all those great memories and remember what it's like, and still is, to be a Monster Kid!

Halloween Jack

The Monster Channel

INTRODUCTION

There is a certain disease that affects some of us. It doesn't have a vaccine. No over-the-counter drugs can combat it. No one can perform an intervention and deprogram us. It's an addiction to watching horror and science fiction movies. If I could give the disease a name I would, but so many names would work. Monster Mania. Monsteritis. St. Bela's Disease. Whatever it is, I got it, which is why I'm writing yet another book about my favorite film actors and the movies they appear in.

I've already put forth *Dr. Dreck's B-Movie Museum*, followed by *Monster Kidding*, *Lurking in the Late Night*, and a fiction work *Escape from the Domain*, (all available online both in print and as an ebook). My Dr. Dreck persona has enabled me to dig up all kinds of obscure and borderline movie spookers, which I gleefully present on my long-running TV show, *The Dungeon of Dr. Dreck*. I like to champion these oft-maligned movies and let each viewer decide whether or not they have any merit. Little did I know when I started the program, along with my co-host, Lorna

Nogueira, that I would end up writing books about them. But here I am again.

I won't snow you; this is not serious film criticism, these are just my observations on the films presented in this book. I'm just a fan. I won't get all artsy fartsy and try to find deep meaning in *Manos, the Hand of Fate*. Think of this book as just you and I sitting around in the living room, talking about our favorite subject, MONSTERS!

YOU COLLECT WHAT?

This will make no sense to anyone born after cable television changed the way everyone watches TV programs. Back in the day, (we old-timers like to talk like that), one of the most popular magazines in America was the digest-sized TV Guide. Every week you could pick up your region's copy of the guide at the store or supermarket, and at your leisure, peruse that week's offerings by the big three networks, ABC, NBC, and CBS. Later on, you would start to see additional channels pop up. These were the UHF stations. You needed a special TV and antenna to pull in these stations. But here's the rub that seems inconceivable nowadays; you could only watch any given show on the day and time it was broadcast. You couldn't record it to see it later or pull a show or movie up via ON DEMAND. No Netflix, Prime Video, or any streaming service. Wild, huh?

As a kid, getting ahold of the weekly TV Guide every week was even better than getting the oversized Sears Christmas catalog. My young eyes became a movie detector, scanning each page looking for the elusive horror flick I hadn't seen yet, hoping and praying it wasn't on in the middle of the night, or worse, on a TV station you couldn't get. My family would get the eastern New England edition, which listed some channels in New Hampshire and Connecticut. We couldn't get any of those stations where I lived in central Massachusetts, so it was really frustrating to see movies pop up on those channels.

Now that I'm in my dotage, (I'm pushing 70 as I write this), I discovered that I get a childlike thrill looking at an old TV guide from the 1960s, which to me is the highlight decade of my childhood. I love seeing the listings for Friday and Saturday nights. A wave of nostalgia overwhelms me when I see a listing for Fantasmic Features, Chillerama, and Chiller. On some occasions, I vividly remember watching a particular movie at that time, such as Horrors of the Black Museum. I'll never forget the first time I saw the binoculars scene. A woman gets a gift from an unknown admirer. She pulls out a pair of binoculars from the box and looks through the eyepieces. Sprong! Two metal spikes plunge into her eyeballs. The thing is, you never see it, you just see the bloody binoculars on the floor and see the screaming woman covering her eyes with blood dripping down her cheeks. I bought the TV Guide dated on the night I first saw that movie. Friday night, 11:30, Chiller on channel 12 in Providence.

More than a few times I would spot a movie that was on at one o'clock in the morning during a school night, so my brother and I would set an alarm and turn on the TV in our room and watch it. Most of the time I needed two toothpicks to keep my eyelids open.

So yes, maybe this seems goofy to most people to cherish old TV Guides enough to buy them, but the nostalgic trip I take whenever I open a vintage one, is worth every penny I paid for it.

CASTLE OF FUN

I love William Castle's films. I can't claim to have seen all of them, but the ones I have seen are a joy. His gimmicks may be his main claim to fame, but his legend wouldn't still be going if that's all there was to it.

We know he started with Columbia Studios directing The Whistler movie series and an early Robert Mitchum movie, When Strangers Marry. But it wasn't until his first film, titled Macabre, that the William Castle we know and love would come into his own.

Macabre was his first gimmick movie. If anyone died of fright during the showing of the film, Lloyds of London would

pay $1000 to the deceased's family. Nobody croaked as far as I know. Although the star of Macabre is William Prince, I paid more attention to Jim Backus. To me he had always been Mr. Magoo and Thurston Howell on Gilligan's Island, so seeing him in a straight part kind of threw me. Same thing when I finally saw Rebel Without a Cause. I would never have imagined James Dean and Mr. Magoo in the same film.

Macabre was based on a kind of round-robin novel, The Marble Forest, written by several writers under a single pseudonym. It's all about a fake kidnapping of a child who is presumably buried alive so it's a race against the clock to find where she's buried. A decent film, but has none of the flairs of the later Castle films. Still, it's the starting point of the Castle gimmicks galore era and noteworthy for that.

House on Haunted Hill is usually a fave for Castle fans. It certainly is mine. I was never fortunate enough to see this film in

the theater so I missed out on "Emergo". A fake skeleton was rigged up behind a black curtain near the screen, and at the right time, it flew out over the audience. Once it became known to movie-goers, it was only a matter of time before some wiseacres would be waiting to throw things at it as it passed over them.

What a cast. Vincent Price is at the height of his powers as the suave and sinister Mr. Lauren. His biting exchanges with his wife, Annabelle, played by Carol Ohmart, are one of the many highlights. Elisha Cook, who made a career out of being a scared weasel, is also a big plus in the cast. His line as they go into their rooms for the night is a gem. "What's the use of saying Good Night?" Cook actually survives in this movie, which is kind of a rarity for him.

The first time I saw this one was on a UHF station during the 60s. It had two standout moments for me. When the lead woman, Nora Manning, played by Carolyn Craig, is locked in a darkened room, she turns to see the woman caretaker, Mrs. Slyeds, standing behind her. We get a close-up of her snarling face, and she literally "slides" by Nora and out of the room. If you don't expect that shock cut it is quite a jolt. I know I was scared by it. Also eerie is when the same hapless heroine is in her room and the apparition of Price's wife appears at the window. She had supposedly just hung herself, and the rope crawls through the window like a snake and curls around Nora's ankles before retreating into the stormy night. Since all this supernatural jazz is just a fake, I wonder how the two conspirators rigged up such a specialized gag and timed it just right.

The weakest part for me is when Annabelle is pushed into the convenient acid vat in the cellar. The skeleton that corners her looks too flimsy to have the oomph necessary to shove her in.

Sure there are a lot of plot holes, but with a movie like this, the fun of watching it overshadows any shortcomings. I never get tired of watching this one.

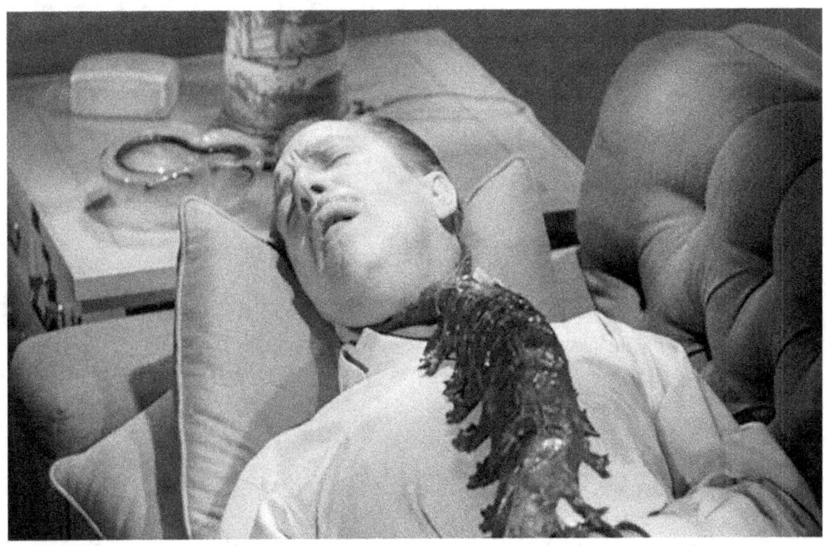

The Tingler is another Price starring role which is my second favorite Castle film. The Tingler is the creepy crawler that is spawned in the spine of a frightened person. It looks kind of like a silverfish without so many legs. If you don't scream in terror, it will kill you.

Oliver and Martha Higgins are theater owners of a downtown revival cinema that shows only silent movies. Martha is a deaf-mute. Oliver is acquainted with Dr. Chapin, (Price). One night he brings his wife's corpse to Dr. Chapin's office. Seems something has scared her to death. Why he brought her to Chapin is anyone's guess. Maybe Chapin has walk-in autopsies. So what happens when a deaf-mute woman is terrified and can't scream? Well, the Tingler sets up housekeeping in the body. Our boy Vincent extracts the nasty beast and boxes it up for safekeeping. Or not so safe. Price's luck in marriage has run afoul again and his shrewish wife sees the Tingler as a good opportunity to dispose of her bothersome hubby. She releases the Tingler while Price is zonked out on the couch. The Tingler crawls up on his chest and starts to strangle him with its front feelers. Price awakens and screams just in time to make the Tingler jump ship. Just as well for the Tingler, since it would be hard for the creature to find a good lawyer if it had succeeded.

A highlight is when Price tries to induce the Tingler in himself by dropping some acid. LSD was still legal at this time, so Vinny must have had a good connection. After he goes under the influence, you would kind of expect a little more in the way of special effects, but what mostly happens is wavering walls and Price's histrionics. "The walls! The walls!" I thought it would be fun to watch this scene with the sound off and play the Beatles song, "Tomorrow Never Knows" during it. I can imagine Price gyrating to "turn off your mind, relax and float downstream."

For Dobie Gillis fans, Darryl Hickman, (Dwayne's older brother), is Price's young assistant. Hickman played the older brother to Dobie in the TV series, but he subsequently disappeared and was never mentioned again. I guess he went to work for Dr. Chapin and the Gillis family didn't want to talk about it.

There is more than one gimmick for this movie. The first one is something I didn't get to see until the movie came out on DVD. It is rather clever and effective. Martha, the theater owner who is a deaf-mute, is experiencing strange and frightening occurrences in her home when she's alone. She closes herself in the bathroom. The movie was shot in black and white. It appears to still be black and white until she looks at the bathtub. It is filled with blood. Thick, red blood. A hand comes out of the tub covered with it. This trick was accomplished by having a black and white set, with the Martha character wearing grey scale clothing and her face and hands made up as grey. Since the scene was shot on color film, you do notice a subtle shift in the film grain when it cuts to and from it.

The big-time gimmick for this was the closing scenes in the silent movie theater. The Tingler wasn't happy being trapped in a box at Oliver's house, so it escapes. Oliver's apartment is right above their movie theater, so the Tingler makes its way in without buying a ticket. As most monster kids know, selected seats were wired with buzzers underneath. When the film being projected appears to break, we see the Tingler crawling across the white void. The lights go out and we hear Price imploring the audience to scream for their lives. The projectionist in the real theater would hit the switch to activate the buzzers. Lucky patrons unaware of the gimmick would get their butts buzzed. It would have been so much fun to be in the theater to witness this.

Karma catches up with Oliver at the end, as he was the one who frightened his wife to death with trickery. At the apartment, Chapin puts the Tingler back into Martha's body. Oliver confesses his guilt, and Chapin leaves, presumably to tell the police. Martha, however, gets re-animated and comes back from the dead to get her revenge on Oliver, who is too scared stiff to scream.

Homicidal is probably the ultimate in Castle weirdness. Trying to outdo Psycho with a cross-dressing maniac, star Jean Arliss, (Joan Marshall) is not too convincing in her "male" outfit. Even if you don't know the gimmick, you can tell the voice is dubbed in, and you have an odd-looking man, to say the least. As a side note, Marshall was in the pilot episode of The Munsters as Phoebe Munster, but never made it to the final casting. One of Castle's bloodier efforts, as we have the mad woman carving up

a Justice of the Peace and cutting off the head of an elderly woman she is taking care of.

One of the more amusing gimmicks for this movie is the "Fright Break," where skittish patrons who couldn't stand the scary ending could go out into the lobby and stand in the Cowards' Corner. It might have been fun just to do that.

13 Ghosts is a barrel of undead fun. The gimmick for this one is the Ghost Viewers. When the ghosts appeared on the screen, the black and white movie turned into two colors. Wrongly thought of as 3D, what the viewers actually did was enable you to see the ghosts more clearly or not at all. The main set was tinted blue with the ghost images overlaid in a red tint. I had cousins who saw it in the theater but they didn't keep the viewers.

Old Hollywood standby Donald Woods plays Dr. Zorba, (no,

not Ben Casey's pal), who inherits ghost viewers from a crazy uncle who collects ghosts. We are treated to each of them in turn via the ghost viewers. Adam 12 star Martin Milner takes an evil twist in the road from the straight and narrow and is the villain of this piece. Throw in Margaret Hamilton, (the Witch from the Wizard of Oz), for color and you have a fun night in the theater or just on your couch with a bowl of popcorn on your lap.

Mr. Sardonicus is a more subdued Castle flick. Guy Rolfe is the titular character. Based on a story by Ray Russell, Mr. Sardonicus has a bad case of Joker smile due to his greed.

His father died and was buried with a winning lottery ticket in his coat. Sardonicus can't stand his penny ante life and digs up the old guy. When he opens the coffin and sees his father's decaying rictus face, his face freezes into that same ghastly smile. Character actor Oscar Homolka plays Krull, and when he's not assisting Sardonicus with his schemes, he has fun putting leeches on a bound-up servant girl. The gimmick for this one is the Punishment Poll. Supposedly there were two endings shot for the movie. The audience was supposed to vote with cards distributed to them whether it was thumbs up or down to spare Sardonicus's life. There was no alternate ending shot where Sardonicus lived. Castle knew everyone would want to lower the boom on Sardonicus, not to mention the improbability of the theater projectionist having to deal with a quick switch.

The Old Dark House is probably the most maligned of Castle's films, perhaps unfairly. If you're going to compare it to

James Whale's classic with Karloff, then yeah, there's no comparison. Look at it as a standalone comedy, and it isn't bad at all. Castle wasn't really a comedy director, but he had a good cast for laughs in this one. Tom Poston is the star, supported by Brits Robert Morley, Peter Bull, (in two parts), and Joyce Grenfell as Aunt Agatha. The emphasis is on humor and not much of the scary stuff. The murders are amusing, especially Grenfell's, who is killed with her knitting needles shoved through her neck. Morley's character remarks it must be murder because Agatha was always so careful with her knitting. Poston is an everyman kind of character which to me adds to his appeal. When I saw the movie in the theater it was in black and white. It was released to TV in color. This was similar to another film I saw in the theater, The Frozen Dead. Black and white prints were distributed to the theater, but the telecasts were in color. Go figure.

Strait-Jacket almost transcends its B movie roots by starring Joan Crawford. She had just scored big time in Whatever Happened to Baby Jane? The screenplay for this one is by Robert Bloch. The cast includes early performances of George Kennedy and an uncredited cameo by Lee Majors.

Castle had to cater to Crawford's every whim to get her onboard. No matter what year it was, she always saw herself as a major star. To her credit, she lets herself be seen looking her age

as a recently released mental patient. In a flashback we see her catch her cheating husband in bed with another woman. She comes across an ax and then…chop, chop. Two heads gone.

Her daughter, played by Diane Baker, is nervous about Mommy Dearest coming home, but she tries to be a good daughter to her under the circumstances. Before long, people start losing their heads. George Kennedy as the slimy caretaker gets the extreme haircut, and later on, a doctor from the asylum gets axed in the barn. SPOILER: Yeah, you're right. The daughter is bug nutty and she's doing it.

That's the biggest flaw in the script. Crawford's character is made to look guilty as sin at every turn. She's not just a red herring, she's a maroon herring. There's no other person that could be the killer, so you figure out pretty quickly it's the daughter. A mystery this isn't.

Fairly graphic for its time, it features four beheadings. The first two are seen in shadow, but Kennedy's character buys the farm in full view of the audience. There's a technical flaw in the scene, though. They are using a very good dummy head of Kennedy attached to a body that squirts blood. Special effects were advanced enough at the time to make life masks of actors to add realism. As he leans over a box, the axe comes down on him. The problem is, the shot is just a little too long before the ax hits him in close-up. You have time to see that it is a dummy head. A tighter edit would have been more effective, cutting right at the point where the ax hits his neck. Oh, well.

However much a pain she may have been, Crawford gives a wonderful performance.

Zotz was another Castle comedy. Tom Poston stars again as the absent-minded professor type. Jim Backus returns to a Castle film, this time in a comic role. A special treat in this one is the appearance of Margaret Dumont in a party scene. You expect Rufus T. Firefly to walk in any minute.

The Zotz coin was a giveaway to patrons of the theater. In the

film, the ancient coin had mystical powers. If you have the coin on your person, when you point your finger at someone, they experience excruciating pain until you lower your hand. If you simply say the word, "Zotz", whatever you're looking at starts to move in slow motion. If you point and say Zotz at the same time…Uh oh! You just killed somebody. I kind of wish I had this coin and it worked. I wouldn't kill anyone, but I know some people…

For aging baby boomers, you'll get a special kick out of seeing Louis Nye in a bit part. Nye, along with Poston, Gabe Dell, and Don Knotts were part of the old Steve Allen show.

The Night Walker is a whole lot of fun and has enough of a creepy story to keep you going. The great cast stars Barbara Stanwyck, Robert Taylor, Lloyd Bochner, and Hayden Rorke.

Stanwyck plays Irene Trent, who is married to Howard, an insanely jealous man. He's also blind and has a makeup job that

doesn't quite make him the sexiest man alive. Although blind, Howard has an upstairs laboratory in which he works on secret projects. I don't know how a blind guy can conduct experiments alone. One night he makes a mistake and gets blown up real good.

Irene has a recurring dream of a fantasy lover, (Lloyd Bochner), who carts her around town and knocks her off her dreamy feet. The family lawyer, Barry Morland, (Robert Taylor), is concerned about Irene's mental stability. Irene's dreams become more and more frightening, culminating in a "wedding" ceremony in an eerie church. The priest, organist, and guests are all mannequins. The recorded voice of the priest is somehow both gentle and ominous. But someone has an objection to the wedding. Howard enters, looking the worse for wear and Irene freaks out.

It all turns out to be a plot to drive Irene to either kill herself or drive her over the edge. Lawyer Barry fixed Howard's will to make him the beneficiary. I guess Howard had blind faith in lawyers. There's a lesson there. Howard gets bumped off with a rigged explosion, and the dream man has been hired to help Irene lose her mind. All ends well though, with the bad guys fighting each other and falling through a hole in the floor of the lab. Irene stands alone at the end.

I enjoy this one a lot. I saw it in the drive-in when it came out. The scariest thing was Hayden Rorke, both before and after the explosion. Hard to recognize him as the actor who played Dr. Bellows in I Dream of Jeannie. Sharp-eyed viewers should look for the brief part of a gardener that Irene encounters. The actor is Tetsu Komai, who played M'Ling in Island of Lost Souls. We also have the great Paul Frees doing some sinister narration at the beginning about nightmares with cool images. There was a paperback version of the movie by Bloch, also.

Castle made some black comedies such as The Busy Body, The Spirit is Willing, and Let's Kill Uncle. I still prefer his version of The Old Dark House as his best black comedy. Besides, Charles Addams did the title artwork!

These aren't all the Castle films, but if you're looking for the cream of the creepy crop, try these on for size.

IF I HAD A HAMMER

I've never understood the battle between which studio turned out the better horror films, Hammer or Universal? The output of the two giants of horror/sci-fi cinema is so different from each other that it's pointless. I think I could safely say that if Universal never started the classic horror cycle, then Hammer wouldn't have taken it up in the 50s.

If you want to identify who turned out the most "classic" horror films, then Universal did, mostly because they had more time to do it. But Hammer scored some great ones too, only more graphic and in color. Universal's classic monsters, Dracula, Frankenstein, the Wolf Man, and the Mummy were all later recycled in England, the first two faring better than the rest. I'll give you my opinion on the standout Hammer flicks.

I think in terms of a series of films with a recurring character, most people would pick the Dracula pictures with Christopher Lee as the best series. However, I disagree here. I think the best Hammer series wasn't horror at all, it was science fiction. I pick the Quatermass series as the all-around best series. All three pictures stand out as intelligently written, well acted, and thoroughly involving.

The Quatermass Xperiment, (in the US it was The Creeping Unknown), started the ball rolling in 1955. The deal was that an

American actor in the lead would give the film a better chance in the states. Nigel Kneale, who wrote all three screenplays in the Quatermass series, didn't like Brian Donlevy in the role. He may have thought he just wasn't right for the part or had heard about Donlevy's drinking problem. If Donlevy had a problem with alcohol it doesn't show in the movie, as he always seems to be a commanding presence, not someone who can barely walk straight.

A standout performance is given by Richard Wordsworth as the doomed astronaut, Carroon. Without uttering a word, the actor's struggle with the alien form consuming his body elicits pity rather than terror from the audience. There's even a "Frankenstein" moment as Carroon is met by a little girl, Jane Asher after he escapes from the lab. Fortunately for the girl, he doesn't harm her although there is a moment of suspense where he is trying to control himself. Wordsworth had two other notable roles in Hammer films. He appeared in The Revenge of Frankenstein as the jovial assistant in Frankenstein's free clinic, and as the beggar in Curse of the Werewolf.

The Quatermass Xperiment plays like a documentary with stark black and white photography and real locations. The final view of what Carroon has become is effective, though brief. The music is by the great James Bernard, one of the unsung heroes of many Hammer productions.

Quatermass II, (US: Enemy from Space), finds the determined Quatermass investigating a mess of meteorites hitting the earth. While handling some fragments he and his assistant Marsh find by the side of the road, one of them sizzles and burns

Marsh's face. Suddenly a goon squad dressed in black takes Marsh away despite Quatermass's protests.

Quatermass discovers that a secret complex, Winnerden Flats, is where Marsh was taken. Not one to give up, Quatermass contrives to enter the facility to find out what's going on.

Shot in the same style as Quatermass Xperiment, some viewers think this sequel is better than the original. I think I concur with that. It's the kind of movie that doesn't stop for a second.

The alien menace is a big pile of pulsating muck, which is growing by the minute. Fortunately, Quartermass saves the day.

The third Quatermass movie came years later. This time we have a new Quatermass and the movie is in color. Quatermass and the Pit, (Five Million Miles to Earth in the US), is my favorite in the series and the most thought-provoking. Andrew Keir is a less abrasive but no less effective Quatermass. This saga raises the question of whether the human race is the product of seeding from another planet. It touches on our conception of the image of the devil. The harrowing conclusion shows the city inhabitants possessed by some alien force. They go on a rampage, attacking each other, and it is only through the sacrifice of a brave scientist, played by James McDonald, that a complete disaster is averted.

The cast is also graced by the presence of the lovely, Barbara

Shelley, as Barbara Judd. She is momentarily possessed by the alien intelligence.

The crown jewel of Hammer's output is undoubtedly Horror of Dracula. Everything came together perfectly for this film. A superb, athletic Van Helsing in Peter Cushing, and a savage, inhuman Dracula in Christopher Lee. Great support from Michael Gough, Melissa Stripling, and Carol Marsh.

Let's face it, no movie version is very faithful to the novel, and this one lacks a Renfield and kills off the book's main protagonist, Jonathan Harker! That doesn't take away from the movie, which keeps up the pace and excitement throughout. Unfortunately, Hammer never hit the height of this classic again, although Lee kept returning as Dracula in progressively weaker sequels.

Lee does get to speak in his opening scenes, but after that, all bets are off and his teeth kick into high gear. The climax is one of the great vampire killings in movies. According to legend, Peter Cushing came up with the idea of using candlesticks as a cross. He also did the 100-yard table dash himself. Impressive.

EXCEPT…my choice for second place as the best Hammer vampire movie is Brides of Dracula. Not really a sequel, but an offshoot. Its big plus is the return of Cushing as Van Helsing. David Peel is a vampiric disciple named Baron Meinster, and although totally different from Lee in manner and appearance, he is still very effective in the role. He strikes me as a vampiric Dorian Gray.

Van Helsing goes the extra mile when he has to barbecue his neck after Baron Meinster bites him. Cushing does it so

convincingly you almost feel it.

This movie also breaks from what Van Helsing said in Horror of Dracula, i.e. vampires can't transform into bats. Baron Meinster has no trouble changing into a big flapping bat, so I guess he didn't read the handbook. But if he can change into a bat, why didn't he free himself from the ankle chain which imprisoned him previously? In my previous book, Monster Kidding, I made a guess that the ankle brace was made of silver, so he was powerless to change. He is destroyed in an offbeat manner. Van Helsing jumps on a windmill blade so its shadow throws the image of a cross on the ground, right where Baron Meinster is standing. He doesn't like that a bit, but he can't move. He collapses and presumably dies. Brides and Horror are the two most action-packed Hammer films. Unfortunately, a lot of the later ones are more talk than action.

For my money, the third best Hammer vampire film is Kiss of the Vampire. A honeymooning couple gets stranded on a country road when their car runs out of gas, oh, I mean petrol. Little do they know that the evil Dr. Ravna (Noel Willman), is eyeing them through his telescope in his nearby castle. Gerald, (Edward DeSousa) and his wife, Marianne, (Jennifer Daniel), find a place to stay at the local inn. They receive an invitation to a dinner at Ravna's castle. They have a charming dinner with Ravna, his son, and his daughter. Ravna neglects to mention that

he's a vampire and oh, yes, he heads a cult.

Kiss of the Vampire puts a Transylvanian twist on things. Next, they accept an invitation from Rava's castle to attend a masked ball. During the party, Gerald gets tanked up on booze and passes out. The next day when he looks for his wife in the castle, Ravna and his two blood-starved children, pull the shell game on him and deny the existence of Marianne. Then they throw Gerald out in true vampire hospitality.

I enjoy this movie for a different kind of take on vampirism, as it delves into the more cultish aspects of it. Ravna has a gaggle of blood drinkers at his place, and he intends to indoctrinate Marianne.

Gerald enlists the aid of Professor Zimmer, (Clifford Evans), who lost his daughter to the cult. We saw Zimmer at the start of the movie as he stood beside his daughter's grave as her coffin was being lowered into it. Zimmer broke ceremonial protocol by picking up a shovel and thrusting it down through the lid of the coffin. Now to show you how faulty a kid's memory can be, I had thought the coffin had spewed a few buckets of blood out of the lid, filling up the hole. In actuality, just a good amount of blood oozes out, but not enough to fill the hole.

The climax has been dissed by reviewers, but I thought it was thrilling and scary at the time. Zimmer conducts a ritual that calls up a battalion of vampire bats to break into the castle and destroy the vampire cult. I guess human vampires can't trust vampire bats. Yes, of course, the effects aren't anything like they could be done today, you can see they are rubber bats, but I don't think it spoils the movie.

They finally got Christopher Lee back for Dracula, Prince of Darkness. Lee was also the prince of silence as he doesn't utter a word in the whole film. There are conflicting stories about why. One side claims it was that way in the script at the beginning, but Lee had said the dialogue was so bad he refused to say it. No matter, since he doesn't have to play nice to fool anyone, it's good that he just gets to be himself.

We have the typical stranded Brit tourists, who seek refuge in Dracula's castle, much to their regret.

Barbara Shelley is a standout in the cast as a very prim and proper lady until Lee puts the bite on her. Then she's one hot bloodsucker, looking for either gender to make a blood donation. Equally creepy is Phillip Latham as Klove, the stone-faced butler. His memorable scene involves hanging a man upside down and cutting his throat, so the blood pours into Dracula's stone bed. For once we can see that Dracula would be naked in that coffin when he's revived as we see his unclothed arm grope the side of the tomb. Although he managed to put on his ring somehow.

No Peter Cushing this time, so we make do with Father Sandor played by Andrew Kier. Kier was an excellent Quatermass, and he makes an admirable substitute for Cushing. Thorley Walters plays an ersatz Renfield, as the loon who lives in an abbey. He's there to invite Dracula into the abbey, following the vampire rulebook.

In a scene right out of the book, Dracula corners the heroine, played by Suzan Farmer. He slits his chest open with his fingernail and tries to force her to drink his blood. She gets even with him at the end, though. She shoots at Dracula while he's standing on an icy moat. Water starts to burble out which makes Sandor remember that vampires can't pass running water. A few more potshots at the ice and Dracula sinks slowly in the sunset, er, water.

Dracula Has Risen from the Grave was next. Lee got to talk in this one and he's as nasty as ever. To allay the fears of the villagers, the new Monsignor of the town, (Rupert Davies), along with the village priest, performs an exorcism on Dracula's castle, which makes the vampire persona non grata. The village priest is a jellyfish and refuses to go all the way up Drac mountain. When the ritual is completed, the scared priest runs away. He loses his footing and falls, hitting his head on a rock. Blood drips from his head onto the ice. Guess who's under the ice? Dracula, naturally. All he needs is a little taste of the hemoglobin and he's ready to rock and roll.

His new servant is now the former priest who is scared Godless of Dracula. Since Dracula needs something to occupy his time, he decides to get revenge on the Monsignor.

With the help of the priest, he secures a coffin and makes himself at home in the basement of a bakery, which is under a tavern. Dracula quickly makes a slave of one of the tavern girls. Plan 9 for Dracula is to get even with the Monsignor by vampirizing his, of course, beautiful daughter, played by Veronica Carlson.

I think the goofy thing about this movie is when Dracula is staked he pulls the stake out because the young guy skewering him is an atheist. The requirements for staking vampires got a little more stringent with this opus.

All in all, this is a decent one in the series because it tries to be different.

Taste the Blood of Dracula is something else. Originally, Lee turned it down. Hammer recruited Ralph Bates to be a disciple to fill in the hole. But the US distributor said, no Lee, no distribution. Hammer threw more greenbacks at Lee, so the original plan was scuttled. Although Dracula is barely in it, the idea behind it is unique. Lord Courtley, played by Bates, recruits some upper-crust crumb bums looking for a thrill, to help him revive Dracula. After putting some fresh blood in a goblet of Dracula dust, Courtley demands the men drink from it. They refuse so he chugs it himself. It doesn't go down well, as Courtley falls to the ground, screaming bloody murder. He grabs at the legs of some of the men, so they kick and beat him to death. Then they all scram to their safe little homes. Ah, but the ritual worked. The corpse of Courtley transforms into Dracula. Now it's revenge time, folks. Dracula hides out in an abandoned church, where he methodically arranges the deaths of the four rotten guys, using their own children to do the killing.

Two different things about this film. First, you're on Dracula's side, because the guys he has killed deserve it. Dracula's death is unusual. When the nominal hero re-sanctifies the church by placing a cross in the doorway and arranging the altar properly, Dracula starts freaking out and falls onto the altar, where he then dissolves into dust.

Scars of Dracula qualifies as the most brutal of the series.

Dracula stabs one of his vampire women multiple times and presses a hot poker onto his servant's back as punishment for disobeying him. Lee gets to talk more in this one, somewhat resembling his manner in the first movie before he revealed his true nature to Harker. A lightning bolt finishes him this time, causing him to do a fiery free fall off the castle roof. It's kind of amusing to see that his servant is played by Patrick Troughton, the second Doctor Who.

Dracula A.D. 1970 is to me, the nadir of the series. I agree with Christopher Lee that bringing Dracula out of his gothic trappings into the modern world was a bad idea. Of course, the money that Lee pocketed wasn't a bad idea for him. The best thing about the movie is that it brings back Peter Cushing.

This film doesn't even try to connect to the previous one. We are treated to a prologue death of Dracula by a descendant of Van Helsing. A hundred years later a disciple of Dracula, named Johnny Alucard, (ooh! clever name) gathers the dust to resurrect him. He gets a bunch of young people to help him in a ritual to bring Drac back. A desecrated church is in the neighborhood, so that's as good a place as any for black magic rituals. When Dracula returns from the dust heap, he wants revenge on Van Helsing's descendants, in this case, Lorrimer Van Helsing. Making a vampire out of his granddaughter, Jessica seems like a good idea. Johnny volunteers to become a vampire, (what a guy!), so he can help Dracula on equal terms.

Lorrimer, who figures out Alucard is Dracula spelled backward, tracks Alucard to his flat. The two fight and in one of the strangest vampire deaths, Alucard is killed when he falls into a bathtub and accidentally hits the shower faucet. The running water destroys him.

Van Helsing sets up a nice pit of wooden stakes near the church. Dracula has already put the bite on Jessica, who is doing her zombie best to obey him. Once the vampire king is outside, Van Helsing throws holy water into Dracula's face. That blinds him and he falls on the stakes, but not far enough. Van Helsing picks up a shovel and pushes Dracula further into the stakes. Ouch.

The film has dated badly as do many films that tried to capture an era. Lee has little to do, and Alucard is more obnoxious than anything. We do get to see the beautiful Caroline Munro before she moved into other Hammer projects.

The last film featuring Lee as Dracula ended up with different titles depending on who distributed it. I'll go with The Satanic Rites of Dracula. Although this one is also based in the present, it fares much better than the previous one, and the plot line is a mix of horror and James Bond-like intrigue.

Cushing returns as the same descendent of Van Helsing. Lee gets to do something different, as he masquerades as a Howard

Hughes-type recluse named D.D. Denham. His scene with Cushing in the office is a highlight. Van Helsing has made a silver bullet that he hopes to drill Dracula with. Lee adopts an accent for his character as Denham. But Van Helsing exposes Lee by turning around a desk lamp into Dracula's face. Van Helsing isn't fast enough to use the silver bullet though, as Dracula's henchmen subdue him.

Van Helsing speculates that Dracula has a death wish, which is why he sponsors a cult that wants to spread the bubonic plague throughout the world. I guess Dracula figures if all the humans are dead, he'll die of starvation. You would think he'd prefer the stake or the sun.

This time Dracula expires when he is caught in hawthorn bushes. Once he is snagged, Van Helsing breaks off a fence post and impales him.

Lee finally made good on his word to not be Dracula again. The Legend of the Seven Golden Vampires is one wacky hybrid of martial arts and horror. What little of Dracula is seen is played by John Forbes-Robertson, but even having three names is not enough to compensate for Lee's absence. We do have Cushing back for his final go at Van Helsing. It's unique, I'll say this for it. The Chinese version of "hopping vampires" is rather an eerie sight. Plenty of action unfolds, both of the socko variety and the vampire killings.

A family of brothers aid Van Helsing to track down Dracula who has taken the form of a Taoist monk. Seems the Temple of the Seven Golden Vampires is having power problems, and the hapless monk enlists Dracula's aid in putting them in the driver's seat again.

If you're in the right frame of mind, you can enjoy this movie, if, for nothing else, the blending of two different genres. Hammer drove the final nail into Dracula's coffin with this one. From this point on they swiveled to the Carmilla series of films.

The other long-running Hammer series was the Frankenstein saga. As we all know, the series centered on the doctor rather than his creations. Having Peter Cushing as the star of each installment was the best thing about them.

I've never had a great affection for the Hammer Frankenstein series. I don't think they're bad; I just think they're erratic in the way they portray Baron Frankenstein. Sometimes he's an evil bastard, other times he's rather like an anti-hero, and sometimes, as in a couple of others, he seems downright sympathetic.

The Curse of Frankenstein started it all and propelled both Peter Cushing and Christopher Lee into monster super-stardom. If Lee had not been cast as the creature in this one, I don't think he would have ever ended up being Dracula.

Okay, to start off with my kvetching, I liked Lee's creature during the first half. His makeup is certainly distinctive, and his tall stature and black wardrobe complete the package. Where the movie falls down for me, is that after the creature has escaped and is terrorizing the countryside as all good monsters do, Frankenstein and his assistant, Paul, shoot the monster in the head. From that point on, Lee's creature is just a half-bald, pathetic puppet. As a monster, he's almost negligible. I wish the movie had been more about Frankenstein pursuing the monster to stop his rampage, which would have been like the novel. Shelly's Victor Frankenstein chases his creation to the ends of the earth. It also would have beefed up Lee's part and perhaps allowed him the opportunity to instill a little more humanity into his role. Hazel Court plays Victor's finance, but she doesn't have much to do, other than look beautiful, which she always does effortlessly.

Cushing is at his most malevolent in this movie, and the

movie ends with him coming face to face with a guillotine. Anyone who'd rather play around with monsters rather than Hazel Court deserves to have his head cut off.

I think my favorite one is The Revenge of Frankenstein. Again, there is barely a monster in this one, as the poor guy who has his brain transferred to a pre-fab body is more to be pitied than anything.

Frankenstein escaped the guillotine from the first movie, which apparently was such a good switcharoo of bodies that we don't get to see it, only hear it.

Dr. Stein, (guess who), runs a charity hospital. When he's not helping the sick, he helps himself to their body parts when he needs them. His new assistant, Hans, knows who he really is, but is so in awe of Frankenstein he won't snitch on him. Dr. Stein is prepping to put the brain of his deformed assistant, Karl, into a new model, made from parts he's accumulated. The brain switch works, and Karl awakes in a new, improved body, (Michael Gwynn). Karl hates his old body so much that he takes it and shoves it into the basement furnace. A big oaf caretaker catches him at it and takes advantage of Karl's initial timidity, by punching him out and smashing a chair over Karl's head. Uh oh, wrong move. The concussion loosens some cogs in Karl's brain and he turns bestial and murders the big goon.

In short, Karl runs amuck and while he's a-mucking, his

physical appearance deteriorates until he starts to resemble his old body. He tracks Frankenstein down and bursts in on a social gathering, where he shouts out Frankenstein by name, spilling the beans on Dr. Stein's identity. He falls dead into Frankenstein's arms.

Now that everyone knows who he is, Frankenstein is attacked by his patients in his charity ward, where they nearly beat him to death. But Dr. Stein had a backup plan for just such an event. He already had a backup body waiting for him. Hans performs the operation successfully, and we see the recycled body introduced as Dr. Frank. I suppose his next body would be Dr. En.

Cushing is excellent as always, and Francis Matthews gives his usual sturdy support as Hans. Michael Gwynn is especially touching as Karl, and even though his mental processes go haywire, we still pity the poor guy.

I think I have a soft spot for this one because, in my youth, I had the 8mm version of this movie which I watched numerous times. Although it was in black and white, I thought the editors did a good job cutting the film to a ten-minute length.

The next movie, The Evil of Frankenstein, threw caution to the wind and didn't even try to tie in with the first two films. Cushing is still pretty tame this time around and even tries to prevent an evil hypnotist, played with slimy glee by Peter Woodthorpe, from using the monster to get revenge on his enemies.

Since Universal was able to give their blessing to this go-around, they didn't have to steer clear of the Karloff makeup. Unfortunately, they botched it. The monster's forehead looks like a square cardboard box. Combined with grey makeup, strands of black hair, and blackened eyes, the monster looks less human than any of the previous monsters. Having a non-actor play the creature doesn't help either, although I don't know how any actor could elicit any pathos in that kind of get-up.

This creation was a previous experiment of Frankenstein that got loose, fell into a cave, and was frozen. Where this monster charts in the parade of monster misfits is anyone's guess. With the help of a deaf-mute girl they befriend, the monster is found and is ready for defrosting.

Since Frankenstein and his assistant, yet another guy named Hans, have nothing better to do, they chip the monster out of the ice and try to reanimate him. But the monster's brain is in permanent pause mode. Frankenstein and Hans find a sleazy hypnotist, Zoltan, at a local carnival and proposition him to jump-start the monster's brain. That's when everything goes to hell. A more fitting title would have been The Evil of Zoltan since he's the real bad guy in this. After Zoltan gets skewered with a metal lance by the monster, the whole shebang goes up in flames when the monster flies into a rage.

Despite all my grousing, I still like this movie. I like it better than the last two in the series, which may be blasphemy, but that's me. Mr. Blasphemy.

Baron Frankenstein goes metaphysical with Frankenstein Created Woman. He wants to isolate the human soul, with the help of his assistant, Dr. Hertz, (Thorley Walters). The Baron believes he can capture the soul and then transfer it to another body. His other assistant is a young man named Hans. (Are there no end of Hans's in these towns?) This Hans is the lover of a young girl, Christine, played by Susan Denberg. Christine works in her father's tavern, and because of her facial deformity is ridiculed by three upper-class twits. Hans gets into a fight with them, but Kleve, the owner of the tavern, throws them out. Not to be deterred from being a bunch of jerks, the three creeps return at night and break in to steal wine. Kleve catches them in the act and they beat him to death. Hans had been in bed with Christine at the time and didn't know what happened, but when he arrives at the inn the next day, he is immediately pegged for the murder. I guess first come, first arrested. His alibi is Christine, but to protect her honor he clams up. So Hans faces the guillotine and gets the big haircut. A distraught Christine drowns herself in the lake. The Baron and Dr. Hertz meanwhile take charge of Hans's body, both pieces, and they isolate his soul. As it turns out, this is Frankenstein's lucky day, as Christine's body is brought to the doctors to see if they can do anything. Boy, do they. They transfer Hans's soul to Christine, then give the girl a major makeover. Hans's spirit has his own plans though and possesses Christine to knock off the three jerks that got him sentenced to death. After the deeds are done, Christine runs to the river bank with Frankenstein in pursuit. Now that the revenge is complete, she has nothing to live for, so she drowns herself again. The Baron sadly walks away.

I think Cushing in this one gives one of his most sensitive performances, and his interaction with Walters makes them seem like a paranormal version of Holmes and Watson. Ironically, they have both played those roles, just not with each other. Denberg's voice is dubbed in, Hammer would do a lot of that with actors, but it looks like she is more than capable of acting the part going by her demeanor. It probably is the most melancholy ending in all of the series.

The next installment, Frankenstein Must Be Destroyed, is one where I feel alone in not liking the film. The Baron does a complete turnaround in this movie, becoming 100% evil. He kicks things off by chopping off the head of a guy so he'll have something to work with. When he's discovered he takes off and gets himself lodging in a rooming house. He wastes no time in insulting his fellow roomers and then proceeds to blackmail the landlady's daughter, Anna, played by Veronica Carlson. Seems

Anna's beau, Karl, (Simon Ward), has been stealing narcotics from the hospital he works in, to give to Anna's ailing mother. Now the Baron has two involuntary helpers for his next plot. Dr. Brandt, who was an assistant to the Baron in earlier days, went nuts and is locked in an asylum. Not wanting to do anything the easy way, the Baron wants to kidnap Brandt so he can get some secret formula he has sitting in his brain. Brandt ruins the plan by having a heart attack, so now the Baron and his pals kidnap the head of the asylum, Dr. Ritchter, (Freddie Jones). The Baron pops Brandt's brain into Richter's skull. Richter not only has a new brain but a new personality as well. The original Richter was a pompous jerk, but now he's a completely sane good guy.

As if the Baron wasn't despicable enough already, he then suddenly rapes Anna. This vile scene was demanded by the producers against the wishes of Cushing, Carlson, and director Terrance Fisher.

Richter awakes and scares Anna, who stabs him. He escapes and goes to his wife who of course won't recognize him. The Baron gets teed off at Anna for stabbing Richter, so he stabs her.

The Baron goes to Richter's house, figuring, where else could he go? Richter wants revenge, so he gets his wife out of the house, so he can set up a big bonfire with Frankenstein as the guest of honor. Frankenstein shows up and gets the papers for the formula he wants, but is intercepted by another unhappy person,

Karl, who discovered that Anna is dead. They fight, but Richter appears, conks out Karl, and hauls Frankenstein into the burning house, presumably until he is done on both sides.

I have no complaints about the production or the acting, which is usually good to excellent in Hammer films, it's the nasty script I don't like. Frankenstein, even when he's committing crimes, from the second movie on, had a kind of anti-hero air about him, but it's completely trashed in this film and there's no one to root for. I'm used to seeing Freddie Jones in seedy or creepy roles, so it was nice to see him do a turnaround in his personality. The last two Frankenstein movies are, for me, not conducive to repeated viewings.

Frankenstein and the Monster from Hell wind up the series for good. No Frankenstein versus the Kung Fu Pandas or anything like that.

I like this one better than FMBD. Although Frankenstein is still a sociopath, he's in the place where he belongs; an asylum for the criminally insane. He's not an inmate though. He's blackmailing the actual head of the place, Klauss, who had attempted to rape his own daughter, Sarah. The girl suffers from shock and is mute. Dr. Victor keeps her near him as an assistant. Klauss lets him have the run of the place posing as Dr. Victor. Well, he already used up Dr. Stein and Dr. Frank, so I guess Victor is still good.

A young man, Simon, is arrested and thrown into the asylum after he's caught collecting body parts for his experiments. Dr. Victor, seeing in Simon a like-minded medico, enlists him to assist on his monster-making project. Not one to waste opportunities, Dr. Victor uses patients at the hospital to involuntarily donate to the cause. Dr. Victor procures a body, a pair of hands, eyes, and a brain right from his fellow inmates, without having to call a mail-order monster shop. Things don't work out, of course. The newly formed patchwork of people parts is not too happy about the situation, especially when he looks in a mirror and sees the kisser he's stuck with. The monster also overheard what Klauss had tried with his daughter, and the creature seeks him out. He finds Klauss in his office, breaks a large bottle, and shoves it into Klauss' throat. He then sets his sites on more mayhem. The creature is finally killed by a couple of bullets fired by an attendant, and the rest of the crazies who can roam about at will, inexplicably tear the monster to pieces.

Dr. Victor shrugs off his newest failure and returns to his lab, telling Simon and Sarah that after they clean up the mess, he can start again. I guess this fits in with the definition of insanity; doing the same thing over and over but expecting a different result.

Several things stand out in this film. Cushing, who is getting on in years at this point, is more gaunt than usual, and they gave him a rather curly, gray-haired wig, which gives him sort of a foppish look. No matter, Cushing never gives a bad performance. He's pretty subdued in this one, although he can be commanding when the need arises.

We also have the most graphic footage of a brain transplant this time around. Saw off the top of one head, snip, snip, the ocular nerves, snip, snip, the spinal cord from the brain stem, then reverse the order in the recipient. It looks as easy as replacing the batteries in a flashlight. Some gross humor occurs during the transplant. After Cushing removes the bad brain, he throws it on the floor in a pan. Then he trips over it and the brain and blood get spilled all over the place. Just another fun day in body-building class.

The weirdest aspect of this whole thing is the "host" body. An inmate who had killed himself had been dug up by Dr. Victor, and he is the creature we see throughout. Dr. Victor says the guy was a throwback, and he's not kidding. He looks like a hybrid of a man and a gorilla. His barrel-chested torso and shoulders are covered with hair, and his face looks like he was the last in line when they gave out faces. How this guy previously walked around in polite society seems far-fetched.

So we come to the end of the Quatermass, Frankenstein, and Dracula series. If I had to pick the best film out of the bunch, it would be Horror of Dracula. If I had to pick the best series, I would choose Quatermass. Granted, there were only three of the Quatermass movies, but all three are top-notch.

Hammer only made one notable werewolf movie, Curse of the Werewolf, but I'm tempted to call it Curse of the Where Wolf? As I carped about it in Monster Kidding, they had this great werewolf makeup for Oliver Reed, but you don't see it until the last few minutes. What a waste.

Hammer made three mummy movies. The first, The Mummy, starred Christopher Lee in his only turn as the bandaged one. This version relied more on the Kharis series of Universal Studios. One big difference though is that Lee's Mummy is fast on the kill, so no one has to stand there waiting for the Mummy to drag himself over to them. This is the best Mummy version, as the other two, Curse of the Mummy's Tomb, and The Mummy's Shroud, were pretty dull and the mummy action was pretty scarce.

There were Hammer one-offs over the years, such as Plague of the Zombies, The Reptile, The Gorgon, and The Phantom of the Opera. I think Plague is the best of the bunch. Having Andre Morrell in the lead and some good shock scenes made it a more rewarding viewing experience. In Phantom, they completely abandoned the monstrous aspect of the character, and although well played by Herbert Lom, the only mayhem is perpetrated by a mute servant of the Phantom. The Phantom is even the hero of the piece at the end, as he sacrifices himself to save the heroine's life from a falling chandelier. Michael Gough is the real villain, playing Lord Ambrose, who steals the music the Phantom has written. What's astounding is that he never pays for his crimes. He unmasks the Phantom and runs away, but escapes unpunished. I like to think that when he ran out into the street he got run over by a horse and carriage.

FRANKENSTEIN MONSTER MUG SHOTS

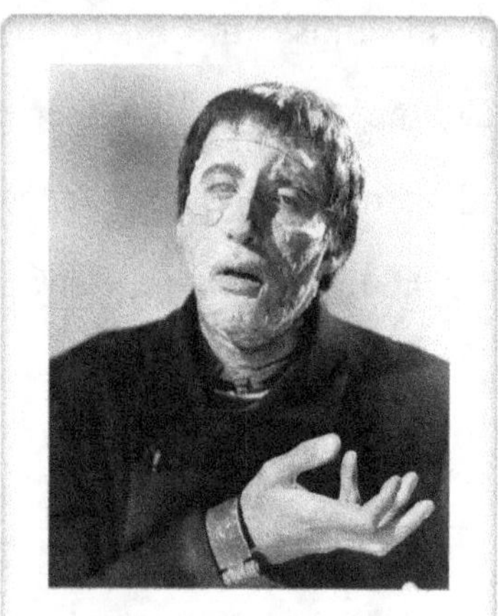

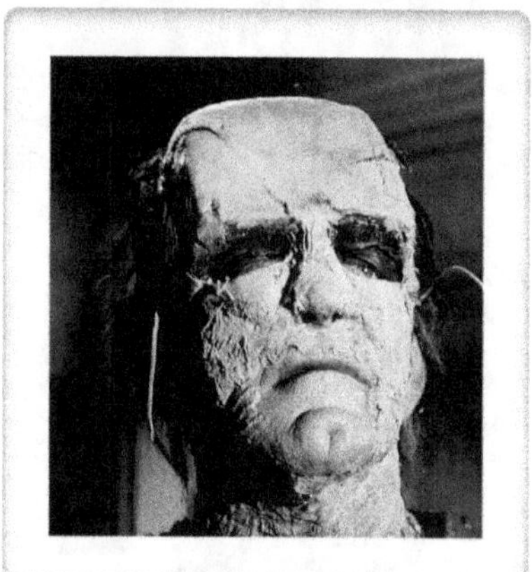

I WANT MY UHF

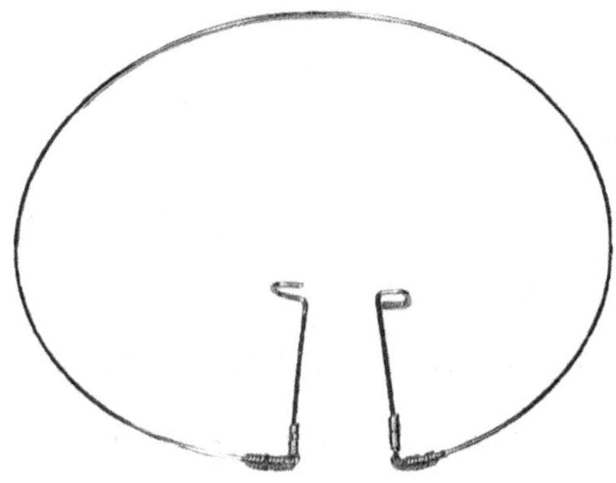

It's old geezer time! If you were born during the age of cable and endless channels to choose from, consider this a history lesson.

My growing-up era was the 50s and 60s. TV was very simple then. It operated on what was known as "very high frequency" or VHF. By way of illustration, I'll use my own experience to demonstrate. Where I live, (Massachusetts), we had six or seven stations that our valiant outdoor antenna could pull in. The big three were CBS, NBC, and ABC, and the educational channel, PBS, which I never watched. Who wanted to be educated when you were six years old? We had four stations out of Boston and two out of Rhode Island; channels 2, 4, 5, 7, 10, and 12. Depending on the weather and a lot of luck, we could pull in channel 6 out of New Bedford, and even channel 9 from New Hampshire! Wow! And that's it, kiddies. Can you believe how primitive we were? I mean, really. But who knew what the future would bring? However, around the mid-60s, the future did bring something new called "ultra high frequency" or UHF. New independent stations started to crop up. One problem though, most existing TV sets, including our big box in the living room, couldn't pick up those stations. You needed a new TV with a separate dial and a separate antenna. It was kind of like having your old transistor radio that only had AM, and FM suddenly became the place to be.

Eventually a little, teeny weeny TV came into a house. This baby could get UHF. Instead of the old-fashioned "rabbit ear" antennas, UHF required a loop antenna. See how high-tech we were?

My brother and I had to huddle around this little screen, which I think couldn't be more than 6 inches wide. It wasn't much, but a whole new world opened up. Three stations popped up in our state, channels 56, 38, and 27. The first show I remember seeing is Soupy Sales, and best yet, one of the stations ran all the Sherlock Holmes movies on Sunday nights. Luckily the movies were short because we had to go to school the next day.

Eventually, every set in the house was replaced with dual receiver TVs, but you still had to contend with the damn antenna and the weak signals from the UHF stations. The little guys of

UHF couldn't show any of the network programming, so they ran old movies, syndicated shows, and hosted kiddie shows with cartoons.

The best thing to come out of the new wave of UHF stations was the Creature Double Feature! The heyday of the horror-hosted shows had just passed by, although one Boston station did run classic horror on Saturday nights. Creature Double Feature, which was channel 56 in our area, bounced around on the schedule. It was Friday nights, then Saturday nights at prime time, but finally settled on Saturday afternoons. They ran through the classic Universals and some B movies, but then they seemed to concentrate on Toho movies. I like a lot of the Toho movies myself, but I never could get into all the Godzilla sequels that were aimed at kids.

That was the vast wasteland we old timers lived in. More miracles were to come. I was flabbergasted when I got my first VHS recorder and could record and keep movies to see whenever I wanted! Then DVD players, cable, Roku streaming devices... AARGH! The six-year-old me would have never believed it. In some way, I still don't.

HOLMES HORRORS

In 1939, the Fox studio started production on the first American sound film to feature Sherlock Holmes. They made two great decisions. They picked the most famous Conan Doyle novel, The Hound of the Baskervilles, and they cast a pair of actors that would be identified with the roles for decades to come. Basil Rathbone as Holmes and Nigel Bruce as Watson, proved to have an onscreen chemistry that made them beloved by moviegoers. The two Fox features kept the time period of the original stories. In The Adventures of Sherlock Holmes, they introduced supervillain, Professor Moriarty, portrayed by old neon eyes, George Zucco. Watson as played by Bruce was denigrated by purists as being too buffoonish, but he is a more serious chap in the Fox films.

For some reason, Fox didn't continue the series, but fortunately for us, Universal started their franchise, snagging Rathbone and Bruce to play the roles. Although the Universal series of 14 films were made by their B unit, the studio gloss is still apparent and doesn't show any cheapness at all.

Out of the films, some of them are borderline horror movies, although there is no supernatural element. You could say that any movie with murder in it is a horror movie, but I'm choosing the ones that have the most spooky elements.

I have no problem with Bruce being the comic relief in these films. If they portrayed Watson as seriously as they portrayed Holmes, it might have made for heavy going, at least for the time period they were made in.

In the House of Fear, the film takes a premise from a Doyle story, The Five Orange Pips, as a jumping-off point for what is basically an old dark house thriller. A group of friends who call themselves the Good Comrades, start receiving envelopes with the orange pips in them. Soon after a member gets the pips, he gets pipped, I mean, knocked off. And not just in any conventional way. One drives off a cliff, one is burned to a crispy critter and another is blown up real good. Holmes and Watson are hired to investigate, along with the typically bumbling Lestrade, played by Dennis Hoey.

I won't give away endings in case you haven't seen the films, which I highly recommend. There's a long but amusing sequence that takes place during the night while a wild storm buffets the house. Watson is on guard in the main room, so a lot of the humor comes from him getting overzealous with his gun, and running back and forth as someone knocks on the front door.

Two of the Good Comrades are actors you will see pop up in other Holmes features. Paul Cavanaugh and Harry Cording were the go-to supporting players in Universal's B movies and it's always a treat to see them.

The murders, although not shown, are particularly gruesome and one shudders to think how they'd be handled today.

The next feature, The Spider Woman, a fan favorite, features the icy but charming Gale Sondergaard as the titular character. Men with a gambling debt are being killed off for their insurance money, but the murders are made to look like suicide by guess who? The Spider Woman! And who collects the insurance money? Right again! Same dame!

The film starts with Holmes faking his death, and the scene with Watson and Lestrade, when they believe Holmes to be dead, is rather touching. Holmes disguises himself as Rajni Singh, an Indian officer, who is supposedly up to his turban in gambling debts. His scene with the Spider Woman when he gives himself away shows that Holmes is not so infallible.

There's not much spooky stuff going on, other than a deadly spider trying a nighttime attack on Holmes, (a variation on the Holmes story, The Speckled Band).

We also get to see a blackened Angelo Risitto playing a pygmy, in a role you'd never see today.

The final scene takes place at a carnival. At the shooting gallery we get to see depictions of Hitler and Mussolini as targets. Talk about real monsters.

The Pearl of Death is one of the classic Holmes entries, even being somewhat faithful to the Doyle story, The Six Napoleons. Miles Mander and Evelyn Ankers make a fine pair of villains, trying to track down the Borgia Pearl. Charles Conover, (Mander), after stealing the pearl from a museum, ducks into a plaster casting shop and pushes the pearl into one of the line of Napoleon busts. Things get complicated when the busts are sold, and Conover has to track down the owners. The big attraction here is Rondo Hatton, making his first memorable appearance as the Creeper. The script wisely keeps him mute, and his formidable presence is all that's needed. It's interesting to note that this is one of the few times where Holmes appears visibly frightened as the Creeper creeps in on him. As a bit of trivia, the Creeper had a prototype in the original story, a big, ugly galoot named Beppo. So Rondo plays Beppo, indirectly.

Throw Lestrade into the mix and we have a great cast of villains and heroes. I'm also grateful that after the first few Holmes entries, they got away from the WW2 themes and went into more sinister plots and characters.

My all-time favorite though is The Scarlet Claw. This entry is the closest thing to a horror film in the Holmes series. Holmes and Watson are in Canada, where their attention is diverted to the gruesome death of Lady Penrose. Her throat was torn out by what the superstitious villagers believe is the monster of La Mort Rouge. Of course, Holmes doesn't believe it, and he and Watson start putting the puzzle together. Special effects wizard John Fulton gets to employ the same glowing figure effect that was used in The Invisible Ray and Man Made Monster, in a scene where Watson is confronted by the monster while walking in the marshes.

The cast is a who's who of character actors: Miles Mander, Ian Wolfe, Paul Cavanaugh, and Arthur Hohl. Special props, though, to Gerald Hamer, who gets the meatiest role of his career as the killer. Hamer takes on several guises throughout the film and is convincing in all of them.

I know that in Doyle's stories there never was a real supernatural menace, but I wish, just once. Fortunately, other writers have taken up the challenge and delivered some good Holmes novels where the supernatural is real.

"I SAY, WATSON. DID YOU REMEMBER TO FEED THE GIANT RAT OF SUMATRA TODAY?

NEVER A DELL MOMENT

Oh, what fun it is to read stories of your favorite monsters in comic book form. In the early 60s, Dell Comics published a series of monster comics for monster-mad kids. There were three different sets: one was a retelling of Universal Monsters, the second was movie tie-in comics, and the third was monsters as superheroes, (which I will ignore.)

My favorites, which I still own, are Frankenstein, The Wolf Man, The Mummy, Dracula, and the Creature from the Black

Lagoon comics. If you were expecting just a rehash of the movies, you were mistaken. None of them tried to reproduce the movies, and in some cases wandered far afield.

Out of these, my favorite is the Dracula issue. Although Dracula himself doesn't show up until the last few pages, the comic has a very creepy atmosphere and an interesting storyline. One night Sir Basil

Shawcroft visits his friend, Janos Tesla, an expert on the occult. Shawcroft's son, an artist, went to Transylvania to find inspiration for his paintings. The son encountered a beautiful woman in a cemetery late at night. At that point, the son stopped writing to his father. Tesla feels the son is a victim of a female vampire. Shawcroft scoffs at the notion, but the pair travel to Transylvania to track down the son. Once settled into their rooms at an inn, Shawcroft is stunned when his son appears in the room, looking the worse for wear. He gets his father to travel by coach to the castle of Dracula. Meanwhile, Tesla has heard the conversation and hides on the back of the couch. At the castle, Dracula finally makes an appearance. Dracula and his vampire friends are sick and tired of tracking down victims, so they want a middleman to get the blood for them, namely a doctor, namely Shawcroft! Since his son is now one of the undead, I guess they figure he's sure to say yes. The whole plan goes to pot when Tesla bursts in, repels Dracula with wolfbane, and gets his friend the hell out of there. No vampires are killed this time around, so the son and his bride are still running around in the neighborhood.

Dracula is depicted in the conventional way, tux, cape, black slick hair, etc. No real resemblance to Lugosi or anyone else. Although he only appears at the end, I still list this as my fave of the Dell comics.

Since Dell got licensed to use Universal Studio's likenesses, their Frankenstein comic features a very Boris monster on the cover and throughout the book. There are some similarities to the movie. We have Fritz, the hunchbacked assistant, and Dr. Frankenstein resembles Basil Rathbone. The first part of the comic follows the path of the movie with its grave robbing and lightning being the reanimating factor. Fritz follows his movie progenitor by thrusting a torch into the monster's face. The monster decides he has better places to be and runs away.

After a few mishaps with villagers, Frankenstein and Fritz recapture the monster. Frankenstein reads an article in the news about a big science conference in America, so he decides to pack up the monster and ship it out to America so he can parade his creation to an astonished crowd. His big mistake was taking Fritz with him, who, unlike the movie version of Fritz, is still alive and kicking. As the monster is hypnotized by the doctor to keep him under control, dim bulb Fritz utters the word to reawaken the monster and all hell breaks loose. Yeah, you guessed it. A fire breaks out on the ship, the monster is burned up, and Fritz and Frankenstein are treading water in the ocean, the doctor vowing to never give up. If he had any brains he'd duck Fritz underwater at this point.

Like all the Dell comics, this version is fun to read and is a little more faithful to the movies than the others. The monster is portrayed as Karloff did, a sympathetic figure, and his face is garishly colored yellow and green and he also sports the classic wardrobe.

Really off the beam from the movie is the comic version of The Wolf Man. Just to confuse us kids, the cover shows a transparent image of Lon Chaney's wolf man across the background image of a man being pursued by wolves. No such werewolf appears in the story; not even close.

The storyline has a medical student, Milo, who after graduation goes to his backward village to bring his former neighbors up to date with modern medicine. He finds the villagers are living under the thumb of a strange-looking guy named Vorcla. I am assuming this is the "wolf man" of the story, although he hardly fits the description of a conventional werewolf. He has pointed teeth and ears, bushy eyebrows, and mega sideburns, but he talks normally and doesn't transform into a four-legged wolf. Milo and Vorcla are immediately at odds as the young doctor says that Vorcla's supposed powers don't exist and he sets out to prove that Vorcla is full of wild blueberry muffins. Vorcla is brought to trial and since admitting he's a sorcerer means death, he tells the court he has no powers. So everyone has a good laugh at Vorcla's expense and he loses face in the town. But not for long. Vorcla wasn't conning anyone, he is the real deal and he commands wolves to kill people that have pissed him off during the trial. For Milo, he has a special punishment. Cornering Milo in his home, Vorcla tells the young doctor he is going to make him into a monster like him. How we don't know, but when Milo's fiancé comes a calling he changes into a nasty creep in front of her. Milo's friend from medical school, Albert, has come along for the ride. Albert kills Vorcla by throwing his silver-headed cane into Vorcla's back, killing him. Milo is de-wolfed and everyone is happy.

When I first bought this comic, I was so disappointed that there was no honest-to-goodness werewolf in it, that I took a pen and drew fur onto the characters of Vorcla and Milo to make them look like I wanted them to. Fortunately, later on, I bought it again and didn't deface it. I have it in my possession to this day. Time has made me appreciate it more, but it does have a supernatural angle to it, even if it completely ignores all the werewolf folklore.

With the mummy, we have the bandaged one resembling Karloff, but unlike the first movie, he stays wrapped up throughout as Kharis was in the later Mummy series. Kind of two mummies for the price of one. Like the previous comics, this one does not follow any of the movies except for the archaeologist losing his tiny mind after he breaks the seal of the tomb containing the mummy. The mummy, whose name this time around is Ahmed, scares the scientist and stalks off for revenge on the descendants of the jolly people that buried him alive. Just because he practiced black magic; can you imagine? Ahmed has a super duper hypnotic eye in his cranium, and he can hypnotize his victims into killing themselves. Fate catches up with him when he climbs to the top of a pyramid, which is even more crumbly than he is. His foothold gives way and the mummy does a high dive into the sand below. At the bottom, they only find his bandages. Ahmed was way past his expiration date.

This one is particularly enjoyable because it is like an alternate universe where Karloff stayed wrapped throughout the whole movie. As long as you don't want to stick to the original movie, you can enjoy the ride.

The last one is the Creature (from the Black Lagoon). Need I say it? Not much resemblance to the movie, although the creature himself looks just like our beloved Gill Man.

This one has some elements of the movie it came from. Scott Warden, a paleontologist, receives a fossil from one of his colleagues, Ariaga, who is on an expedition into Brazil. After Ariga goes missing, Warden decides to go to Brazil to find him. He has to resort to asking a millionaire adventurer, Dudley Gaustad, to finance the trip. However, with a name like Dudley Gausted, we know this guy is a no-goodnik. He's after treasure and fame, and when Olympic swimmer, Monica Love becomes part of the deal, Gaustad is after her too.

Vargas is the crusty captain of the boat and the team goes off in pursuit of answers. Dirty Dudley recruits two lowlifes to accompany him as they go to the Lake of Death. (Very inviting name, isn't it?) Answers come in the guise of the Creature, who doesn't remember putting a welcome mat out for intruders. We get the creature giving the fish eye to Monica when she goes swimming, one of the few direct nods to the movie. However, moving far afield from the movie, the Creature is wounded by spear guns and captured, after he has knocked off a few people. It ends with the captured creature being taken to "civilization". In the last panel, we see that the Creature was not the only gill creature around, as members of his extended family follow the boat from underwater.

Minor grievances aside, I'm really happy to still have these comics in my collection. Aside from the nostalgia value, instead of reading a rehash of the movies they came from, we have a different spin.

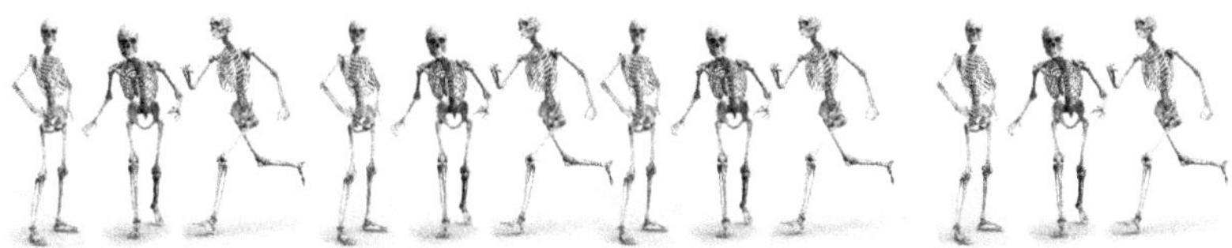

Dell comics didn't stop there. They also released a series of movie tie-ins comics that were faithful to the movies they came from. Most of them are from American International's series of Vincent Price movies, the exception being Twice Told Tales which was released by United Artists.

I foolishly got rid of them in my haste to get money on eBay, and now I wish I didn't. The covers were quite good, and mostly featured photos rather than paintings. Another plus was the artwork resembled the people in the movies, so you got to see Vincent Price and Boris Karloff as comic book figures. During the

60s the comic book market was flooded with horror comics and funny horror comics such as the short-lived comic, Bats. We also had the funny caption monster magazines such as Monsters To Laugh With, and Cracked magazine published many monster issues for us monster crazy kids.

DELL
12c
EDGAR ALLAN POE'S
THE RAVEN
Movie Classic
A STRANGE AND EXCITING STORY OF UNBELIEVABLE MAGIC
mycomicshop
DELL
12c
MOVIE CLASSIC
THE MASQUE OF THE RED DEATH
AUG.-OCT.
DELL
12c
APR.-JUN.
MOVIE CLASSIC
TOMB OF LIGEIA
VINCENT PRICE
BLACK MAGIC CASTS ITS GHOSTLY SPELL WHAT STRANGE AND SINISTER SECRET HAUNTS THIS MAN?!
DELL
12c
MOVIE CLASSIC
DIE, MONSTER, DIE!
ASTOUNDING! STRANGE! WEIRD!
Boris Karloff
AN INCREDIBLE FORCE OF EVIL STRIKES FEAR INTO THE HOUSE AT THE END OF THE WORLD

I would remiss if I didn't mention a different company that filled my childhood with monster memories. Classics Illustrated did quite a few faithful adaptations of famous horror novels. The one that sticks in my memory the most is their version of Frankenstein. When I first saw the comic book cover, I wondered why the monster just looked like an ordinary guy, but inside the book, now that's the monster! I was surprised, and still am, with the gore they got away with. Since these comics were adapted from the books, I knew they wouldn't resemble the movies, but I didn't care. Hey, I was reading CLASSICS! I still don't know why they never covered Dracula.

CLASSICS Illustrated
THE WAR OF THE WORLDS
H. G. Wells
Featuring Stories by the World's Greatest Authors
No. 1
HARDBACK EDITION

CLASSICS Illustrated
THE HUNCHBACK OF NOTRE DAME
VICTOR HUGO
Featuring Stories by the World's Greatest Authors
No. 18   15¢

CLASSICS Illustrated
THE FIRST MEN IN THE MOON
H. G. Wells
Featuring Stories by the World's Greatest Authors
ISSUE No. 41

CLASSICS Illustrated
THE TIME MACHINE
H. G. Wells
Featuring Stories by the World's Greatest Authors
No. 8
HARDBACK EDITION

POE-LIGHT MOVIES

I wonder what Edgar Allan Poe would have made of all the attempts to adapt his short stories. Seeing how he was a literary critic in his time, I can imagine what he'd say. Nothing good, I would wager.

But Edgar, it would be your own fault. Your stories are very moody pieces with a thin narrative running through them. Trying to flesh out a hundred-page screenplay out of a seven-page story is something even you couldn't pull off. Not that people haven't tried.

D. W. Griffith took a crack at it in 1914, when he made The Avenging Conscience, based primarily on Poe's Tell Tale Heart.

Tell Tale Heart is probably the most famous Poe story, so it's no surprise that there are many film versions of it. The first talkie was a British film in 1934. But I will not nail down every single attempt at a Poe story, but instead concentrate on American International's output, which is best known to my readers.

We can thank Roger Corman for getting the ball rolling in splendid style with The House of Usher. Nabbing Vincent Price for the tortured anti-hero was a savvy move, as Price had a grand theatrical acting style that was suited to the florid Poe style. Price's Roderick Usher is a case where Price plays down the theatrics, and with his dyed white hair and soft voice, seems as

fragile as a candle flame.

House of Usher's centerpiece is the specter of premature burial. When a young man named Phillip comes courting Roderick's sister, Madeline, good old Rod is against the union, because the Usher family has a bad case of eventually going nutty as a fruitcake. After an argument with her brother, Madeline collapses into a cataleptic state. Roderick knows she's still alive, but uses the opportunity to bury his sister anyway to forestall any future Ushers. She revives and is not only pissed off but has gone crazy dialed up to 11. She gets out of her tomb and attacks her brother as the Usher house burns to the ground. Phillip makes a getaway hoping for a saner wife in the future.

This is probably one of the most faithful adaptations of a Poe story, the main difference being the narrator of Poe's story is an old friend of Roderick's. As in the movie, Roderick's sister, Madeline falls into a cataleptic trance, and Roderick insists she is entombed. It is vague as to whether he believes she is still alive. In the story, there is no romantic attachment on the narrator's part, so there's no threat of any future little Ushers running through the halls. Madeline does wake up in her tomb and is not unexpectedly off her rocker. She attacks Roderick, the narrator escapes, and the house, which is as cracked as its inhabitants, sinks into the tarn.

Corman initially had trouble pitching the story to the AIP execs because they said there were no monsters. Taking his cue from the story, where Roderick claims the house is alive, Corman said the house is the monster.

A stylish but subdued film, it has a memorably creepy dream sequence, a device that Corman used in subsequent films to jazz up the story. Also, the paintings of the mad Usher kinfolk are cool looking. I could see Rod Serling using them in Night Gallery. The feeling of confinement is heightened by the small cast of four, and almost all the action takes place in the house. I count this film as one of the best Poe adaptations.

Tales of Terror took another direction. Three stories filled the running time, with the second segment being a comedy.

Vincent Price stars in all three segments, with Lorre in the second part, and Basil Rathbone in the third.

Morella is a body switch opus, reminiscent of Ligeia. Price plays Mr. Locke, whose wife, Morella died giving life to their daughter, Leonora. The daughter comes to visit her father, but it's no happy reunion. He blames his daughter for his wife's death. Locke is so wacky that he keeps his wife's decaying corpse in the bedroom. Heaven knows what he does with it. The spirit of Morella rises and kills Leonora, which has the effect of rejuvenating Morella's body. Now Leonora is the one rotting away on the bed. Morella strangles her husband, the place catches fire, Morella returns to her decayed self, and Leonora gets to die with Daddy. I don't know the original story, but I doubt it had a happy ending. This story, although featuring a tortured performance by Price, seems like a tryout for the later Tomb of Ligeia. This segment is a warm-up for the next two stories.

The Black Cat is one of Poe's cruelest stories about a drunken lout who is a nasty piece of work. The movie segment, although titled The Black Cat also appropriates the Poe story, The Cask of Amontillado. Peter Lorre plays the main character, Montresor, the drunken husband of the quite fetching Annabelle, played by Joyce Jameson. They have a pet black cat, naturally. For some reason, Montesor hates his wife and the cat. He didn't know when he was well off. Price plays Luchresi, a prissy wine expert. Montresor and Luchresi have a wine-drinking contest and

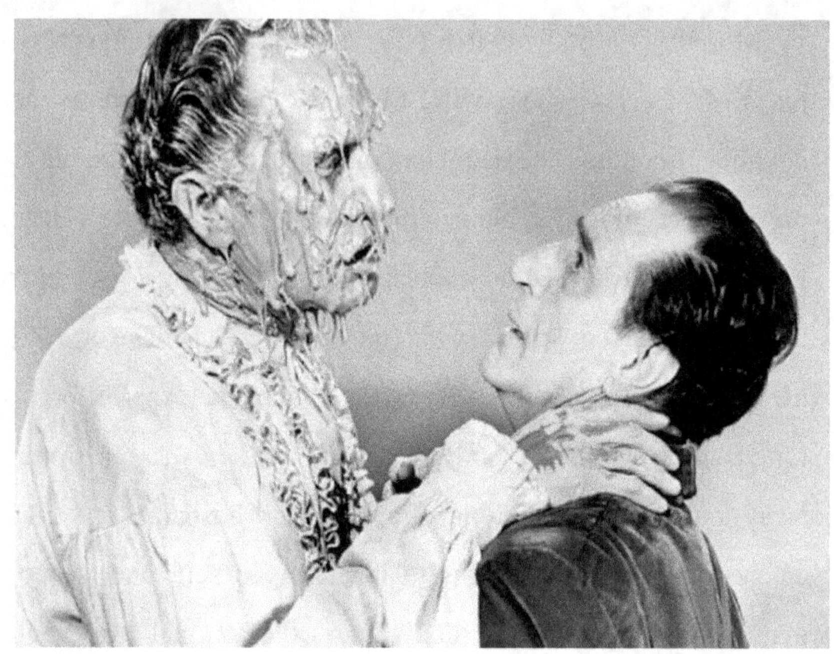

they both get wasted. Montresor brings Luchresi home to recover. Even though he's drunk, Luchresi knows a good thing when he sees it, and he and Annabelle get hot and heavy. Montresor, who up to now didn't care a fig about his wife, is all upset about the affair, so he walls up both Luchresi and Annabelle in the cellar. Of course, he has walled up the cat as well, which howls enough to let the police know that something rotten is going on.

I confess that I have never found drunken people funny. The only exception I can think of is Arthur Houseman in the Laurel and Hardy shorts. So, Lorre's performance and his abusive attitude toward his wife, which is supposed to be funny, just turns me off.

The highlight of the segment is another Corman dream sequence, where they toss Montresor's head around among other things.

The best segment is the last one. Based on one of Poe's gooiest stories, The Facts in the Case of M. Valdemar.

Basil Rathbone, (Carmichael) is the sinister hypnotist that is keeping Price's dying character, Valdemar, suspended between life and death via hypnosis. Unlike the story, the hypnotist has designs on Valdemar's wife, played by Debra Paget. Valdemar begs to be released from his trance so he can die, but Carmichael seems to get off on the power he has over him. Carmichael crosses the line when he attacks Valdemar's wife, which animates the now decaying body of Valdemar to rise and strangle Carmichael to death.

I suppose they had to add Carmichael's lust for the wife to flesh out the story a little and give a more "lively" ending than the original story. In magazines such as Famous Monsters of Filmland, we saw still pictures of Price's character decaying, but it was disappointing in the film because Valdemar's corpse is blurred as it approaches, so we never see a slimy corpse. The makeup Price is wearing looks like it was a good job, so why they blurred it out is lost on me.

The creepiest aspects are when Valdemar is talking in his suspended state. His voice is heard in a stuttering, disembodied way as if speaking from the beyond.

Rathbone gives a good performance as the hypnotist, being as slimy in life as Price is in death. This segment reminded me a lot of what a Night Gallery version of it would be.

Talk about an about-face. The Raven, the next film, turned into a horror/comedy. Hard enough to flesh out a screenplay from a short story, even worse to do the same from a poem. Universal Studios did their The Raven movie, starring Bela Lugosi and Boris Karloff. In that one, Lugosi was a Poe-obsessed madman; I guess you could say he was raven mad. He had a stuffed raven in his study, and he was reciting the poem at the film's beginning. Other than an interlude of a ballet dedicated to Poe, we get off and on references to Poe's Pit and the Pendulum.

Richard Matheson pretty much said to hell with the poem, I'm going to write a comedy. I wouldn't call Matheson adept at writing comedy, but fortunately for all concerned, he had three seasoned horror stars that did know how to play comedy. Vincent Price, Peter Lorre, and Boris Karloff pull off what would be nearly impossible to do with run-of-the-mill bad guys. Their gravitas as iconic horror stars makes the humor that much more pungent.

Lorre's character, a wizard named Dr. Bedlo, has been transformed into a raven by the evil Dr. Scarabus, (Karloff). He

goes to his friend, Dr. Craven, (Price), to help break the spell. Bedlo had challenged Scarabus to a sorcerer's duel, throwing spells at each other. He lost, so Scarabus turned him into a raven. Bedlo claims to have seen the ghost of Craven's lost love, Lenore, (a nod to the poem), at the evil wizard's castle. Both Craven and Bedlo want to lower the boom on Scarabus. It all comes down to an amusing wizard's duel, with Craven winning the contest. And his lost Lenore wasn't so lost; she just shacked up with Scarabus, whom Bedlo had called a dirty old man.

Hazel Court as Lenore is a fair-weather villain, so when Scarabus is defeated by Craven, she throws herself at him, lying that Scarabus had her under a spell. Craven doesn't buy it and leaves her in the castle. If I were Craven, I would have taken her back. I mean, Hazel Court? Of course, I'd want her! What's very odd is to see a young Jack Nicholson as Bedlo's son, Rexford. Who knew what he would become when seeing this movie?

All in all, the movie is an enjoyable jaunt into silly land. When I saw it as a child in the theater, parts of it did scare me, and I think I didn't realize that it was supposed to be funny. Now I know.

For pure over-the-top theatricality, we have Price's performance in The Pit and Pendulum. The only link to the Poe story is the mechanism of the swinging blade and the pit underneath the table where the victims get sliced. Screenwriter Richard Matheson once again had to make a story out of whole cloth.

Beautiful Barbara Steele, just recently off her turn in Black Sunday, is Elizabeth, the deceptive wife of Price's character Nicholas. She's having an affair with Leon, the family doctor, played by Corman regular Anthony Carbone. To drive Nicholas bug nutty, the two lovers contrive to fake Elizabeth's death and then pretend she's haunting Nicholas to drive him mad. Elizabeth's brother, Francis, (John Kerr), ruins the plot by showing up at the castle to find out what happened to his sister. Nicholas's sister, Catherine, and a servant Maximillian don't know about the deception.

The plot works and Nicholas, who was already halfway to loony-ville, finally checks out of reality and imagines he is his

father, who was also betrayed by his wife. His father left him all of his fun torture devices, so the now mad Nicholas wants to give everyone concerned as bad a time as possible. He locks up his wife in an Iron Maiden, although it is not the spiked kind. Nicholas chases Leon off a ledge, so he falls into the pit. Francis, who is without a clue at the time, is knocked silly by Nicholas and awakens to find himself lying under the titular torture device. Francis is saved by the arrival of Maximillian and Catherine, as Nicholas plunges to his death in the pit. Poor Elizabeth is lost in the shuffle and is left to rot in the Iron Maiden.

Price goes from the fragile Nicholas to the sadistic torturer in grand style. You can see that Price is having the time of his life in the second half because it's fun to play a lunatic. The pendulum sequence is handled very well. Low angle shots of the blade and the music score and the swishing sound add to the nervous tension. When we see the blade start to rip through Francis's shirt, we can only hope it's made of rubber. It's hard to garner too much sympathy for Francis. Kerr plays the role as if he'd rather be anyplace else, but the character is sort of a pill as written. Barbara Steele's voice is dubbed, which is too bad, but I guess they thought Elizabeth's voice should have a deeper register. Steele's real voice is much higher and delicate.

A fun movie to watch for Price's performance and the cool dungeon set in the ending sequence.

The Masque of the Red Death is considered one of, if not, the best of the Poe/Corman movies. Perhaps it's because it combines two stories, Masque of the Red Death and Hop Frog. It's a grand-looking film and had the luck of being shot in England where they made use of a leftover castle set from the movie, Becket. Add Daniel Haller's uncredited set design and the cinematography of Nicolas Roeg, and the production proves to be lush and colorful.

The basis of the film follows the story, in that the Red Death is cutting a bloody swath through the countryside. Price plays Prince Prospero, a rich, mean guy who cares nothing for the lower classes. Today that's the requirement for any congressman.

Patrick Magee plays slimy Alfredo, who gets his comeuppance later.

Prospero orders a tainted village to be burned to the ground, but just for laughs, he abducts three villagers, Gina, Ludovico, and Francesca. Prospero has the hots for Francesca, and who could blame him, as she is portrayed by Jane Asher. Prospero's consort, Juliana, (Hazel Court), is far from thrilled by this development and wants to get more into the Satanism jazz to please Prospero.

The other story sandwiched in is based on Poe's story, Hop Frog, a tale of revenge. Two small dancers, Hop Toad and Esmeralda perform for the royal pains during dinner. Esmerelda zigs when she should have zagged, and spills wine onto Alfredo, which prompts the swine to strike her. Hop Toad plans revenge.

After enduring a ceremony to make her a bride of Satan, Juliana ends up getting pecked to death by a falcon. No, not the

Maltese one.

Hop Toad fools Alfredo into dressing up as a gorilla for the Masque ball. He and Hop Toad come into the festivities putting on a show with Hop Toad as the trainer, and Alfredo as the ape. Surprise! Alfredo gets tied up and suspended from the ceiling where he is then set afire by Hop Toad.

During the ball, Prospero espies a guest dressed as the Red Death, so he pursues him through the castle. When he catches up with him, the man turns and we see that it is the real deal, the Red Death, and if that's not bad enough, it has Prospero's face. Prospero thinks this is great and looks forward to all his guests dying except him. Wrong. Prospero becomes a victim as well.

Much more plot to this one, due to the combination of stories. An early draft by Charles Beaumont was turned over to screenwriter R. Wright Campbell, who added the Hop Frog storyline.

I do see two flaws in the movie, one small, and one big. The small woman dancer, who is supposed to be an adult female is played by a little girl, but they made the mistake of dubbing in an older woman's voice which completely ruins the effect. The other flaw is the ending at the ball where everyone dances themselves to death. It seemed hurried and thrown together, and lacked any kind of special effect to make it more surreal.

The Premature Burial is an anomaly among the Poe films.

Instead of Price, the lead is played by Ray Milland, no slouch at dramatics. As in the Poe story, Milland's character, Guy Carrell, is prone to cataleptic fits and is terrified that he may be buried alive.

He has a special tomb constructed with all the bells and whistles necessary to alert people that they jumped the gun on his demise. Little does he know that his wife Emily wants to make sure that Guy gets buried for good and all.

Roger Corman had the rug pulled out from under him when he contracted with Pathe to do this Poe story. Since it was another studio, he couldn't get Price who was under contract to AIP. Hence, Ray Milland steps in. Imagine Roger's surprise when he finds out that the movie is back in AIP's hands, after some underhanded finagling by AIP execs with the Pathe studio.

Like all of the previous Corman gothic films, it is a

handsomely mounted production filmed in Cinemascope. And it does boast a cast of very familiar faces. Aside from Milland, Hazel Court is the treacherous Emily, Alan Napier is Dr. Gault, Heather Angel is Guy's sister, Kate, and the two gravediggers are our old friends, Dick Miller and John Dierkes. Special mention goes to Richard Ney, who amusingly has the name Miles Archer, the name of Sam Spade's ill-fated partner in The Maltese Falcon. His unusual looks made him just right to play the alien Mr. Zeno in the Outer Limits episode, The Special One.

Granted the film doesn't have the pizzazz that Price would have given it, but Milland may have been the better choice since he plays it without getting hammy.

The last of the Poe movies is Tomb of Ligeia, where we welcome back Vincent Price. Once again, the film was shot in

England, taking advantage of the ruins of Castle Acre Priory.

Price plays Verden Fell, who can't get over the death of his first wife, Ligeia. As this is a Poe knockoff, we can't seem to escape black cats, for this film features another feline who seems to be the spirit of Ligeia.

Fell meets the feisty Lady Rowena, and he falls for her. Not a marriage made in heaven though, as Ligeia seeks to possess Rowena. The ending is kind of confusing to me. Ligeia possesses Rowena's body, then she's the cat and scratches out Fell's eyes, then he attacks the cat which turns into Ligeia and the whole furshlugginer mess goes up in flames.

Price has a nice foil in Elizabeth Shepherd, and she is very effective in switching between personalities. The settings are classy as usual, and the castle ruins add a touch of decay.

Although it is not actually a Poe film, I am including The Haunted Palace in this list, mostly because it's my favorite of all these ersatz Poe films.

The only nod to Poe is the title, which is from one of his poems. Price also narrates parts of it in the film. However, this is a Lovecraft story, based on the novella, The Case of Charles Dexter Ward. Charles Beaumont did an admirable adaptation.

Price does double duty: first, he is Joseph Curwen, a warlock who is burned at the stake by the friendly villagers of Arkham, Massachusetts. Naturally, he curses the future generations of the people that burned him up. His ancestor, Charles Dexter Ward, (Price again), returns to claim his ancestral home with his wife, Anne, played by Debra Paget. In an especially creepy scene, they are greeted by some deformed and creepy villagers, the fruits of Curwen's curse on the town.

At the palace, we find Simon, the caretaker, a sinister presence if there ever was one. Maybe because it's Lon Chaney. Also hanging around the place is Milton Parsons as Jabez. He and Simon are former helpers to Curwen in the bad old days.

It's not long before the spirit of Curwen comes knocking on Ward's door, so to speak, as he periodically possesses the usually mild-mannered Ward and turns him into the icy Curwen.

The three warlocks want to raise Curwen's old squeeze, Hester, from the dead. While they're at it, they want to throw

Ann into the pit containing some unspeakable monster from Lovecraft's imagination.

Since people in the town have been getting knocked off left and right, the villagers do what they do best, they storm the castle.

The town doctor rescues Ann while the castle goes up in flames. The portrait of Curwen, which has been the source of all this evil, is consumed by fire, supposedly releasing Ward from its grip. Simon, Jabez, and Hester escape to do bad another day. But is it over? As we see the presumably normal Ward outside the castle, his final facial expression is not that of sweetness and light.

Despite some flaws, I love this movie. The cast is awash with familiar faces: Elisha Cook, (whom you know is doomed the minute you see him), Barboura Morris, Milton Parsons, John Dierkes, Bruno ve Sota, and I. Stanford Jolley.

The big disappointment is seeing the monster from the pit in the final sequence. It's just a still image of some kind of monster, but the image ripples and comes closer while it growls menacingly. Even a few seconds of a stop-motion figure or a puppet would have been an improvement. But it's so seen so briefly that I guess tightwad Roger didn't want to pony up any extra dough.

This film has some of the best opening credits I've seen. A

spider building a web in conjunction with Ronald Stein's ominous score is worth the price of admission. But I'm not picky.

HEARING IS BELIEVING

The theater of the mind. That's what the golden days of radio is called, and rightfully so. Baby boomers like myself are aware of what is called "old-time radio," but many of the later generations may have no idea. Before radio stations became all music or all talk, what ruled the airwaves from the 1930s into the 50s were dramas, comedies, horror, mystery, and science fiction programs. Many featured well-known stars of the day, but most had stock actors where the listener had to supply the face in their imagination.

I became an avid collector of old-time radio shows when I was first introduced to such a thing via an album called, Drop Dead. The LP was produced by Arch Obelor, of Lights Out fame. The album featured short vignettes of imaginative horror, some humorous, some downright unsettling.   A Peter Lorre imitator told us that just because he likes to eat human brains, that doesn't make him a bad person, even though we can hear him sawing through a skull to get at his meal. For people that are dentist phobic, there's a nasty little number of a dentist getting even with a patient of his that's been fooling around with the dentist's wife. Two sketches are standouts. One infamous retelling is of The Chicken Heart which grew to a monstrous size and devoured everything in its path. Unfortunately, I can't hear this one without thinking of vile scumbag Bill Cosby, who made it famous on one of his comedy albums. The wildest cut is called The Dark, about a house where if you enter it, you get turned inside out, along with the gooey sound effects. A lot of LPs came out during the 60s horror boom, which I'll go into later, but first I want to point out the shows that would be of most interest to monster kids.

THE SHADOW: Lamont Cranston, alias the Shadow, is one of the few radio heroes that appeared in pulps, the radio, movies, and even a serial. His powers differed from media to media. In the pulps, he wore all-black clothing and hid in the shadows to surprise his enemies. He also wielded two revolvers which he didn't hesitate to use. The radio show was his most famous incarnation, for it was there that he had the power to cloud men's minds so they could

not see him. His sneering laugh coming out of nowhere was his calling card. The B movies of the Shadow were pretty negligible, as he had no powers at all. The Monogram Studio starred Kane Richmond in three films featuring the character. In the serial, he also had no power to be invisible. Actor Victor Jory looked like how we would have imagined Lamont Cranston to look. The major flaw of the serial, and something totally unnecessary, was Cranston repeatedly assuming the disguise of a Chinese man, complete with all its painfully racist characteristics.

But the radio shows were the best. Orson Welles was the first voice of the Shadow, followed by many others over the years. Many of the stories were spooky or had supernatural trappings.

LIGHTS OUT: Arch Oboler's horror series didn't flinch from portraying graphic depictions of death and murder, and the supernatural aspects weren't explained away. The sound effects made the show. We could delight in the sound of people suffocating, being turned inside out, being decapitated, and all kinds of fun stuff.

SUSPENSE: As the title says, most were suspenseful more than spooky, but they score some good chillers along the way. They tackled The Dunwich Horror, The Birds, Donovan's Brain, and others. This show boasted a lot of prominent stars, such as Orson Welles, Boris Karloff, Vincent Price, Bela Lugosi, and Agnes Moorehead.

INNER SANCTUM: This show featured what would become a staple of horror comics and television programs, the morbidly funny and punny host, in this case, named Raymond. You would think you were hearing an old EC Comic read out loud when Raymond makes his sardonic introductions. Most of the shows didn't venture into horror, but they still had a good stable of actors appearing on episodes such as our favorite fiends, Karloff, Lugosi, Peter Lorre, and Vincent Price.

DIMENSION X: Science fiction came into vogue during the 50s, and radio met the challenge with this program, which later morphed into **X Minus One.** The stories were taken from the masters of the genres, including Ray Bradbury, Poul Anderson, Issac Asimov, Robert Bloch, Robert Heinlein, Fritz Lieber, Philip K. Dick, and too many others to mention. A well-produced and acted show, and though it couldn't boast any name stars in its credits, it stands as the classic science fiction program of old-time radio.

WEIRD CIRCLE: This show was rather different from the others in that the shows were adaptations of famous horror stories. Frankenstein, Dr. Jekyll and Mr. Hyde, and many Poe stories were used on the show. The few novels they did had to be shortened to fit the half-hour time slot. Of special note is the program was produced by ZIV. ZIV became a fixture in television syndicated shows, boasting such classics as Highway

Patrol, Sea Hunt, and Science Fiction Theater.

MERCURY THEATER: Orson Wells radio company didn't specialize in horror or science fiction fare, but will forever be notorious for their Halloween broadcast of War of the Worlds. Welles presented the first half of the show as a series of news bulletins and live broadcasts. People tuning in after the disclaimer at the beginning of the program thought the Martian invasion was the real thing, and panic ensued among some listeners. Such was the power of radio at the time. The Mercury Theater also did an hour-long adaptation of Dracula with Welles as the bloodsucking star.

There were a lot of other programs that had a spooky bent to them. The Mysterious Traveler, The Whistler, Mystery House, Mystery in the Air, Murder at Midnight; but the most far-out one to me is **THE HERMIT'S CAVE**.

The hermit was the show's host, and he kicks off every show with his cackling laughter and opening pitch. "Ghost stories, weird stories, murders too! The hermit knows of them all. Turn out your lights! Turn them off. Have you heard the story of (insert title here)? Eh? Well, listen while the hermit tells you the story!" All this is accompanied by both a howling wind and howling dogs.

I've read that the program was supposed to be tongue-in-cheek, but other than the hermit's over-the-top intros, it seems the bulk of the program is serious. The stories didn't shortchange you either in the supernatural department. Ghosts, vampires, werewolves, you name it, were featured regularly. It's a pity that out of the 800 episodes made, less than 50 still exist.

It's easy to find and listen to old-time radio online. Just search for "old time radio" on the internet and you'll find plenty of programs to stream for free.

Radio drama persisted after its heyday, I will say. The most famous is CBS Mystery Theater, hosted by E.G. Marshall, using his best scary voice.

In the back of Famous Monsters magazine, you could find new LPs of horror stories narrated by some of your favorite people, such as Boris Karloff, (Tales of the Frightened), Basil Rathbone reading Poe stories and Roddy McDowell reading H.P. 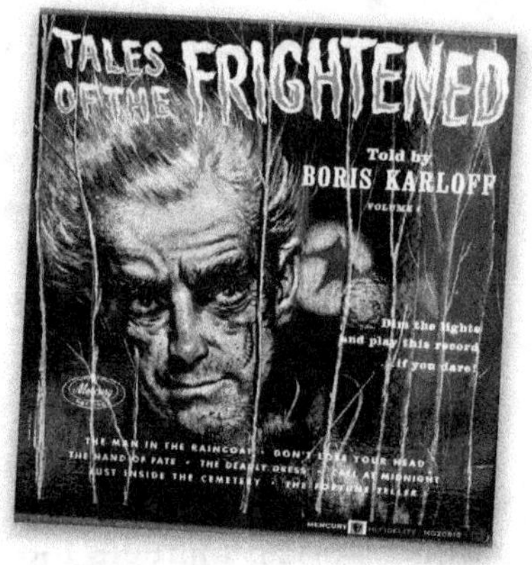

Lovecraft. In addition to the Drop Dead Album, actor/comic Gabe Dell did a double-sided LP of original Dracula and Frankenstein stories. It still is easy to find the infamous War of the World broadcast online.

In 1966 Christopher Lee performed a dramatic version of the Dracula novel on a double LP set. I still own it, although one side

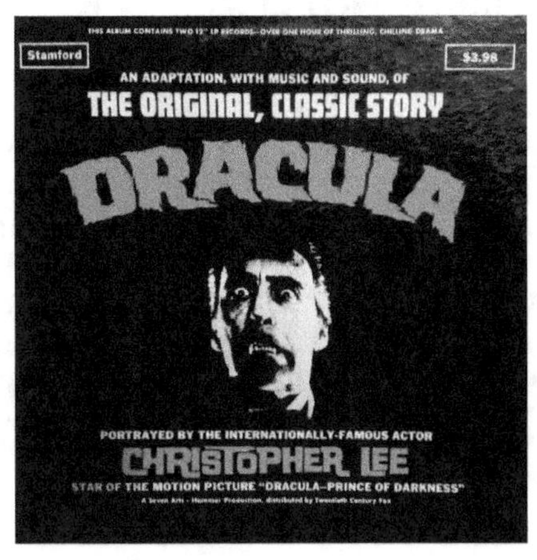

is severely damaged with scratches. Damn,I should have been more careful.

If you're unfamiliar with old-time radio, it is well worth seeking them out. A lot of it can be had for free, but some sellers can sell you loads of mp3s on a disc if you want the physical media. Have a listen. Turning off your lights is optional.

CURSE OF THE MONSTERS

If you're a fan of the old Universal horror films, you'll be acquainted with the following facts. The last "monster rally" film was House of Dracula. A few years later one of the greatest horror comedies of all time came out, Abbott and Costello Meet Frankenstein.

Although I have said in the past that the A & C film is a standalone movie with no relation to the others, I thought I'd try to piece together a movie to form a bridge between these two movies.

I won't give a synopsis of either existing film; you can easily look them up if you haven't seen them. I'm going to take it from where everyone ended up in House of Dracula.

Even though it was his movie, Dracula was killed halfway through the story by having his coffin dragged into the sunlight. Talbot is cured of his affliction by Dr. Edelmann and seemingly will have a relationship with Milizia, Dr. Edelmann's assistant. Before he gets knocked off, Edelmann brings the Frankenstein monster back to life for all of 9 seconds. The villagers burn the joint down and the monster is trapped by falling timbers.

Now, Universal had already thrown continuity out the window at the beginning of HOD. Dracula was turned into a skeleton in the previous movie, House of Frankenstein, and

Talbot was shot by a silver bullet. So, let me explain how they came back in HOD in good health. For Dracula, I have a precedent in other sources.

Dracula's coffin had slid down a hill. Sunlight destroyed Dracula when he couldn't get to his coffin in time. His pursuers, after seeing Dracula reduced to bones, return home, vowing to come back later to properly dispose of the remains. However, they didn't reckon on one thing. That night, when the moon rose it threw its light on Dracula's skeleton, and the moonlight revived him. He changed to a bat and flew away. When the police came back the next morning, they discovered that Dracula was gone.

In the penny dreadful serial, Varney the Vampire, the character is revived by the light of the moon. In Republic Studio's movie Vampire's Ghost, the vampire recovers from wounds when placed in the moonlight. So, this method of reviving a vampire isn't new.

As for Talbot, when he was shot with a silver bullet, the bullet passed through his body, only temporarily affecting him. Okay, that takes care of those guys. Now on to my imaginary movie.

First, I'm giving poor Dwight Frye a few extra years of life so he could appear in this new movie, titled Curse of the Monsters. Here's my dream cast.

Larry Talbot: Lon Chaney

Dracula: Bela Lugosi

Frankenstein monster: Glenn Strange

Peter Van Helsing: Dwight Frye

Milizia: Nan Grey

Mr. McDougal: Frank Ferguson

Inspector Arnst: Lionel Atwill

Instead of a script, I'll give you a synopsis.

Curse of the Monsters

When Dracula was destroyed in HOD, the lid of his coffin, which had been opened to let sunlight fall on him, was left open after Dracula was reduced to bones. After a while, moonlight eventually fell on the open coffin and bathed Dracula's skeleton in its reviving rays. Dracula rises and looks around in the debris of the basement. He detects movement under some fallen timbers. It is the Frankenstein monster, which didn't get destroyed by fire, but fell through the floor and lay dormant while its body healed itself. Dracula helps the monster out of the debris. He sees a potential ally in the monster, as long as he can control him. He hypnotizes the monster to obey him, and is surprised when the monster speaks, saying, "Yes, master." The fall affected the monster's brain giving him limited speech. Dracula remembers that he had almost vampirized Edelmann's assistant, Milizia, when he was interrupted. He doesn't like having his victims get away from him, so he vows to track her down. He remembers that Dr. Neiman, who revived him

previously, had a wagon from a traveling show. The monster and Dracula search the grounds and find it: Professor Lampini's horror exhibits wagon. The monster loads Dracula's coffin in it. Meanwhile, Dracula goes to the village and procures two horses, after killing the owner.

Meanwhile, Talbot and Milizia have traveled to London, where they intend to be married, now that Talbot is cured of his curse. Talbot is disturbed by Milizia's increasing

tendency to fall into a trance at night from which he cannot awaken her, until sunrise. Talbot doesn't realize that Dracula is using his mental link to her, which he had already established, to track her down. The vampire sees in his mind that she is in London.

Dracula abandons Lampini's wagon, and using his hypnotic

powers, wraps the monster in canvas and gets a crate from a shipping company. He has the Frankenstein monster sent to Carfax Abbey, his London abode, which still stands empty. Dracula also puts his coffin into another crate and arranges for

the two crates to be picked up in the morning. Dracula gets into the crate at dawn and leaves a note for the workmen to nail up his crate before they load it on a truck. Dracula and the monster are then transported to London at the same time.

Talbot gets more and more distraught over Milizia's trances and tries to talk to her during them. She finally whispers, Dracula, and Talbot is shocked, believing Dracula dead.

Dracula and the monster arrive at Carfax Abbey. Dracula needs nourishment, but as it is near sun up, he commands the monster to grab a villager for him while he waits in the darkness of the cellar. The monster finds a couple of men, taking a shortcut through the woods to home, after a night of drinking. The monster attacks them, killing one, and knocking the other one unconscious. He drags that one back to the castle. Dracula is pleased and feeds on the victim, then commands the monster to throw the body into the swamp nearby.

The following day, Talbot reads in the paper about a mysterious double murder in the countryside. One man with his neck broken, and another body lying near the edge of the swamp, his blood completely drained. Talbot now knows that Dracula is not dead after all.

The news item also catches the eye of Peter Van Helsing, the son of Abraham Van Helsing. He is also a vampire hunter like his

father. He realizes at once that a vampire is at large, possibly one of Dracula's earlier victims who themselves became a vampire. Van Helsing goes to the police station to question Inspector Arnst about the murders. He learns that the bodies were found not too far from Carfax Abbey. Knowing from his father that Dracula had made it his home, Van Helsing wonders if it is indeed Dracula himself who is committing the murders.

The next night Dracula arises and ventures outside the Abbey. He transforms into a bat and flies to the apartment where Milizia lives. Dracula materializes in the room and hypnotizes her. Taking her by the hand, he leads her back to Carfax Abbey.

Talbot reads that a member of the Van Helsing family was in

town giving a lecture at a university. The news item states that Van Helsing is an authority on vampirism. After contacting the university, he obtains Peter Van Helsing's address. Without revealing his past affliction, he tells Van Helsing that he believes Dracula may still be alive and is trying to claim Milizia, his fiancé, as a victim. Van Helsing asks if Talbot has left her alone in her apartment, and is disturbed that she is unprotected. Talbot phones Milizia's apartment, but she doesn't answer. Alarmed, Talbot and Van Helsing race to the apartment hoping they are not too late.

Dracula has arrived at the Abbey with Milizia. He intends to return to his native Transylvania with her as his vampire bride. In preparation, Dracula still has two wooden crates; one for his coffin, and one to keep the monster in during the journey. Dracula hypnotizes the monster to get in the crate and not awaken until he commands him.

Van Helsing and Talbot arrive at the apartment to find Milizia gone. They decide to go to Carfax Abbey. Van Helsing has a cross and wolfsbane to combat Dracula if he is there. They are unaware that the monster is also there.

As Talbot and Van Helsing make their way into Carfax Abbey, their descent into the cellar is arrested by approaching footsteps. They turn around and see that it is the villager that Dracula had attacked. He had risen as a vampire. Talbot attacks and holds the vampire down as Van Helsing drives a stake through its heart.

The door to the cellar flies open and they see it is Dracula. Dracula turns and locks the door to stall the two men. They break in the door and confront Dracula. Van Helsing pulls out wolfsbane to force Dracula away from the girl, but Dracula commands the monster to awake and attack them. Surprised and defenseless against the monster, Talbot and Van Helsing don't know what to do. Dracula commands the monster to kill Van Helsing, then he turns his hypnotic gaze onto Talbot to freeze him in place. Dracula taunts Talbot so that he can witness Milizia become his slave. Van Helsing lures the monster away but stumbles and falls. The monster picks him up and throws him against the wall, knocking him unconscious. Talbot becomes furious as Dracula goes for Milizia's neck and starts to feed on her blood. The mental stress reactivates his curse and he transforms into the Wolf Man. Dracula calls for the monster to destroy the Wolf Man.

Dracula suddenly realizes it's almost sunrise, and he has no choice but to return to his coffin. Dracula drops Milizia to the floor, as the monster and the Wolf Man fight. As the sun comes up, the Wolf Man becomes human again. With the dawn, Dracula's command of the monster is abated, and the monster goes into a coma.

Talbot goes to Milizia, who is alive, but weak. Talbot checks the reviving Van Helsing. Van Helsing tells Talbot that although a stake through the heart or sunlight will destroy a vampire, there are ways for him to return to life. He says it may be best to trap him in his coffin forever by nailing a cross to the lid and leaving him in this abandoned Abbey. The monster will not rise again as long as Dracula is trapped. They carry the monster over to one of the crates and place the monster inside. Talbot nails the cross to the coffin lid. Van Helsing states he will arrange to rent the Abbey and have the two crates buried deep into the cellar and covered with concrete. The three of them depart. With a heavy heart, Talbot tells Milizia that his curse has returned, and they can't be together.

Unfortunately, the fight with the Frankenstein Monster has taken a toll on Van Helsing, and he suffers a stroke. He never rents the Abbey to bury the two bodies. Talbot goes into seclusion. Six months later the new owner of Carfax Abbey, Mr. Paul Kettering, takes a look at the place and discovers the coffin of Dracula and the monster in a crate. Realizing that they are the real thing, he is frightened to touch them, so he telephones his business partner in Florida, Mr. McDougall.

They realize that the bodies of Dracula and Frankenstein would be a money-making bonanza for them in their new horror exhibit. Both bodies are crated up to be shipped to America. On the way, the crates are handled roughly in transit, and the cross becomes loose but stays in place. Any sudden jolt would shake the cross off the lid and Dracula would be free.

And then, enter Abbott and Costello!

THE SCREENING ROOM

There's no end to the movies I constantly discover buried beneath the mainstream.

STRANGE IMPERSONATION

Republic Studios, one of the classier poverty row studios, made their reputation primarily on the great movie serials they produced such as Captain Marvel, the Dick Tracy series, and King of the Rocketmen. However, they did do feature films and even dabbled in the horror and thriller genre.

Strange Impersonation is a strange film indeed. A mixture of film noir and psychological suspense, the movie seems to constantly veer one way and then another until you don't know how it's all going to end up. But that's on purpose.

Although not the lead, Hillary Brooke in a supporting role is immediately recognizable to monster kids, as the alien-possessed Mom in Invaders from Mars. She was another villain in the Sherlock Holmes movie, Woman in Green. On the other side of the coin, she was the friendly neighbor to Abbott and Costello in their TV show.

Brenda Marshall, who also appeared in the Warner Brothers spooker, The Smiling Ghost, plays the lead character. Nora Goodrich, a research scientist, is developing a new anesthetic that is in the process of being tested. She ends up being blackmailed when she accidentally hits a pedestrian with her car. Add in a jealous co-worker, a love triangle, and disfigurement by acid, and you have quite a bowl of calamity chowder.

You may see the ending coming a mile away, but with the short running time, I don't think you'll find your time wasted. It's a compact little B movie, with good performances and a fun payoff.

Boy, did this one gross me out when I first saw it. Once you see the binoculars scene, you never forget it.

Michael Gough, who excelled at slimy villainy and over-the-top performances, graces this lurid thriller with his presence. He is a crime writer with a unique take on his profession. Commit an atrocious murder, then write about it. No waiting, no taking a number until called. Gough gives new meaning to the word, sociopath.

Gough plays Edmond Bancroft, a big fan of torture devices and an obsession with Scotland Yard's "Black Museum" of murderous tools for the do-it-yourself enthusiast. Crippled in body and mind, he has a cozy little black museum of his own in the basement of his house. He is assisted by a young man, Rick, who is seemingly controlled by the bilious Bancroft.

Joan, (June Cunningham), is Bancroft's mistress. I guess she isn't too picky or she thinks he's some kind of meal ticket. She asks him for money, which leads to a violent argument with Bancroft. She ridicules his physical disability which is not the brightest idea.

Bancroft is also a fan of Robert Louis Stevenson, as he has devised a way to turn his lackey helper into a Mr. Hyde whenever he wants. Bancroft disposes of people he doesn't like in creative ways. The binoculars with spikes in the eyepieces, a portable guillotine that gives the big haircut to his wayward girlfriend as she lies in bed, and performs *tongs for the memory* on a sleazy old woman shopkeeper, using the ice grabber to pierce her neck.

Gough is always so much fun to watch since you know he's having fun emoting all over the place. This was one of three Herman Cohen productions with Gough, the others being Black Zoo and Konga.

In this country they added onto the running time with a silly prologue by a so-called professional hypnotist, Emile Franchele, demonstrating HypnoVista. It had nothing to do with the movie really, but I guess William Castle's gimmick fever was contagious.

During the first half of the 1930s, Lionel Atwill was in the top tier of the most hated villains of the screen. In Mystery of the Wax Museum, he was an insane, disfigured sculptor, in The Vampire Bat, he was a fanatical mad scientist, and in Murders at the Zoo, he was, of all things, a homicidal zoologist!

Spoiler alert: Seeing as the title of the film is the name of Atwill's character, you would think it a foregone conclusion that he is the bad guy. Not true!

Warners Brothers experimented with shooting color film for two of its productions; this one, and the aforementioned Mystery of the Wax Museum. It wasn't the full-fledged Technicolor that later emerged, but sort of a poor cousin. Still, although I usually feel that black and white is better suited to horror films, the garish and primary colors give the two films an eerie look, especially the makeup of the Moon Killer.

The Moon Killer is on the loose, a nut case who not only kills people willy-nilly but cannibalizes them! News reporter, Lee Taylor, is on the lookout for clues and finds himself at the medical academy of Dr. Xavier. The police are also wise to the academy, as the murders were made with a scalpel, not your ordinary butcher knife. We have suspects galore in the academy, and of course, everyone seems guilty of something. Taylor is distracted by Xavier's daughter, Joanne, played by Fay Wray. How could Joanne be the daughter of a psycho killer?

The movie is mostly a lot of fun, with Atwill looking as guilty as sin. Wray doesn't have much to do except give her lungs a workout by screaming. My only gripe is Lee Tracy as the reporter. He's an irritating jerk. The kind of guy that has hand buzzers ready to use, and is equipped with wisecracks. You almost want the Moon Killer to add him to the list.

Still, all in all, catch this one if you can. By the way, it was simultaneously shot in black and white, and the camera placements are slightly different, so there are two versions of this film.

FIEND WITHOUT A FACE

I'll never forget the first time I saw this movie. Still a teenager at the time, I thought the "monster" would always be invisible, which is usually a gyp. Then the last ten minutes came and we saw these flying brains, with a spinal tail and two feelers latching onto people and trying to suck their brains out.

From a short story entitled, The Thought Monster, the movie stars B-movie stalwart, Marshall Thompson. Thompson also graced the productions of It, the Terror from Beyond Space, and First Man into Space. He was a pretty spacey guy. He's at his best in this British production, as he plays hero against the nasty thought monsters. These creatures were formed by a scientist's thought projection experiments, and they are given energy from the radiation leaking from the military radar base. These brainy meanies are like vampires, leaving two punctures at the base of the skull, but instead of blood, they suck out the brains and even the spinal cords of their victims. Yum.

I can't help but think of the Mexican horror film, The Brainiac, who had similar culinary habits.   But where the Brainiac was rather comical, these creatures are bone-chilling scary.

What makes the film is the excellent stop motion of the brains during the climax of the film. They even seem to have a personality. One of them looks curiously at a potential victim before pouncing.

Very effective sound effects are a plus as well. Even before we see the brains, we hear the strange dragging noise they make, and the sound of a quick heartbeat revs up when they start slurping brains. When the visible brains got shot, they make a nice squishy noise as they ooze out blood and gunk.

You'll not forget this movie, you can bet your brain on that.

THE HEAD

During the 50s and 60s, "head" movies were in. I'm talking about the living head of some poor person being kept alive by pseudo-scientific means. The cult classic, Brain That Wouldn't Die is probably the best-known one, but there is also The Thing That Wouldn't Die, The Man Without a Body, and two foreign films, The Living Head, (Mexican), and this one neatly titled The Head, from Germany.

Out of all of them, I would say this one, in particular, has the eeriest atmosphere of not only living head movies but of horror films in general. Just the eerie organ soundtrack alone is shivery stuff, and the fact that the film takes place always at night or in starkly lit interiors, adds an almost surrealistic ambiance to the proceedings.

Horst Frank plays Dr. Ood, a creepy individual with a gaunt face and bushy eyebrows. He reminds me vaguely of actor John Hoyt. Ood is not his real name, but what an alias to use. He finagles himself into a lab run by Professor Abel, played by Michel Simon. Professor Abel is a middle-aged, heavy-set man with a walrus mustache and curly unkempt hair. Soon he will be missing the lower portion of his body.

In this mix is Irene Sandor, (Karin Kernke), a hunchbacked nurse assistant. She is hoping for an operation that will straighten her out. Dr. Ood eyes her and you know there's trouble ahead. Professor Abel, whose heart is ready to call it quits, has developed a serum that will allow him to be the first recipient of a heart transplant. (Who says B-movies can't be predictors of the future?) The mistake he makes is having crazy Dr. Ood operate. The heart transplant fails, so Dr. Ood has a go-to plan. Seems that in the past, Professor Abel kept a severed dog's head alive with his handy dandy serum, so Ood figures, why not? I'll give it a go.

Abel wakes up to find himself the victim of an extreme weight loss program. His head is hooked by wires to machines and bubbling vats. Ood is tickled pink that his experiment worked, but Abel wants him to hit the off switch. Ood says that Abel's great knowledge should be kept alive.

As for Irene who's been waiting to go under the knife, Ood convinces her to let him perform the operation. Ood has another plan than just some minor reconstruction. Ood finds a stripper named Lily in a nightclub that he knows from when he was being crazy under his real name. Ood's plan is put into action. He brings the woman to the clinic, drugs her, and transplants Irene's head onto the stripper's body.

After a few months of convalescence, Irene takes her new body out for a spin. She goes to the nightclub where Lily worked and runs into Lily's former boyfriend, Paul.

To cut to the chase, since Ood has been knocking off people left and right, the police get involved and track Ood back to the clinic. Previously we had seen that Ood was not just an ordinary lunatic. When a full moon rises he freaks out. The moon hits him when the cops arrive, so Ood does a swan dive off a balcony, thus ending his medical career and the movie.

To its credit, I will first say the effect of the living head is very well done. Under Abel's head, we see just a tank and some hoses, creating a believable setup. At times in long shots, it is a dummy head, but the shots where we see Abel and the apparatus are impressive.

As I said, this has a gloomy, creepy atmosphere throughout, and I vividly remember the first time I saw it on TV.

TARGET EARTH

An early sci-fi from Allied Artists. One of the more obscure alien invaders movies, but rather well done with a small cast.

Nora King, (Kathleen Crowley), is the first person we see, and she's not in good shape. She tried to commit suicide with sleeping pills. Having survived that, she discovers that all the utilities are kaput. She goes out to rouse anyone in the building, then goes outside. The streets are deserted; nary a sign of life. She comes across a dead woman lying in an alley and freaks out, backing into Frank Brooks, (Richard Denning). She takes off and he pursues. After she calms down they figure out that during their mutual blackouts, hers from a suicide attempt, and his from being knocked unconscious during a mugging, something dire happened. They both search the deserted city and find two other people, getting drunk out of their skulls in an empty restaurant.

Jim Wilson, (Richard Reeves) and Vicki Harris, (Virginia Grey), aren't sure why the city was evacuated and they don't care. They find out soon enough what's happened, when a frightened survivor, Otis, crashes their party. The group finds a newspaper story about the Earth being attacked by an unknown enemy. Otis, who was already in a frenzy, decides to take off down the street. Then we see the invaders for the first time. A big clunky robot with what looks like a TV tube in its head. Zap goes Otis. Now the four remaining people have to figure out how to stay safe.

To make matters worse, as they are hiding out on an upper floor of a hotel, a sleazy guy armed with a gun forces his way in and takes command. He's an escaped convict and psychopath, and he views the survivors as bait to lure the robots away so he can escape through the sewer system. Vicki gets brave at this point, daring the gunsel to shoot. Bad decision all around. He shoots her dead, and Jim, in a rage strangles the goon.

Meanwhile, our intrepid military and scientists are getting nowhere fast. Whit Bissell, the head research guy, is trying to come up with a way to destroy the robots since regular weapons don't work. They finally hit upon the fact that a certain sound frequency cracks the cathode tube in their head, rendering them inert.

Meanwhile, Frank, Jim, and Nora go to the roof of the hotel, pursued by a slow-moving robot. Once the robot makes his way there, he zaps Jim and is about to fricassee Nora and Frank when an army jeep comes down the street with a huge speaker sending out the killer frequency. Mr. Machine goes down for the count and the Earth is saved.

I saw this movie as a kid and I loved the robot, but then again, I loved all robots. Because of the skimpy budget, only one robot was made. There's a nice shot of the robot's huge shadow against the high rise to add suspense, but I think they could have increased the menace factor more if, by using the same robot, they had a variety of shots of it coming from different places all at once to give the impression of multiple tin guys.

The beginning is very well done, showing the deserted streets of the city. They shot this footage in the early morning on a weekend. Imagine that? No one was around at that time. Nowadays, it seems like everyone is out driving around 24/7.

The cast is good. Richard Denning is always a nice, solid hero, and can make even his hypothesis that the aliens come from Venus seem plausible. Richard Reeves always kind of reminded me of Lon Chaney in build and looks. He usually plays rough characters, some good, some bad. A familiar face in movies and TV, he is always a reliable character actor. Virginia Grey is a long-time working actor. Genre films she appeared in were Unknown Island, (again with Richard Denning), and House of Horrors. Kathleen Crowley also had a long career, but she is most memorable in Curse of the Undead, a vampire western!

What strikes me funny is the fact that the alien robots work by cathode ray tubes. You would think they would have progressed into LCD, at least. I imagine the army jeeps driving around the city with their cathode breaking screeching signal, must have killed every TV set in the area. When the evacuees return, they won't be able to watch television, which they might consider a worse situation than being invaded by aliens.

HOUSE OF HORRORS

I'm sure Rondo Hatton would be amazed to see what an icon he became after death. I'm sure even he didn't fancy himself as an actor, but nevertheless, he has become one of the immortals.

Martin Koslek is the real star of this movie and is responsible for most of the enjoyment of watching it. Although he excelled at playing Nazis, he also played other villains in movies such as The Frozen Ghost, The Mummy's Curse, and The Mad Doctor.

Koslek plays a sculptor, Marcel Delange, who is having a hard time making ends meet; as a matter of fact, he has no ends to begin with. In a twist of irony, as Marcel is about to end it all by drowning himself, he happens to see the Creeper who is beating him to it. Marcel saves the Creeper's life and they become buddies.

Marcel decides to use the Creeper as a revenge machine

against the art critics that have savaged him in the papers. Alan Napier plays a caustic, snide arts writer and he is one of the first to be canceled.

Marcel makes a boo-boo when he creates a sculpture of the Creeper. Joan Medford, played by Virginia Grey, sees the bust of the Creeper and thinks Marcel knows who is doing the world a favor by killing art critics. When confronted with the truth, Marcel claims he intends to turn the Creeper over to the police, not thinking about the fact that ole' Creepy shares the abode with him. Creeper is not happy about his pal turning on him and he kills Marcel. The police arrive in time to shoot the Creeper. But is he dead?

Rondo Hatton certainly looked the part of a monster, but when he opens his mouth a lot of his fearfulness dissipates. Poor Rondo always speaks in a gravely monotone with pretty much no expression. Fortunately, Koslek can do the acting for both of them.

A typical B programmer from Universal still has all the gloss of one of the upper echelon studios. Fast, fun, and even amusing, this House of Horrors is worth the price of admission. And who wouldn't want to own that sculpture of Rondo?

ATTACK OF THE MUSHROOM PEOPLE

Have you ever dreamed of giant mushrooms attacking you? No?

Then you need to see this movie.

In a big departure from his normal type of movie, Japanese director Ishiro Honda helms this surreal, creepy movie.

Based on the short story, The Voice in the Night, by William Hope Hodgson, Honda creates a nightmare landscape of evil fungus among us. A storm shipwrecks several pleasure seekers onto an uninhabited island. There's a mix of character types to give the premise legs. We have a professor and a couple of crewmen, a celebrity, a writer, and a singer, but this ain't no Gilligan's Island. Of course, when you have a group of diverse people, the fur is bound to fly when they're forced to cooperate to survive. Not to mention some garden variety lust on the part of the male survivors toward the female ones.

Food becomes an issue real fast, but although the island is abundant with free-growing mushrooms, the skipper of the yacht warns against eating them, as they might be poisonous. Of course, that restriction doesn't last long when hunger overcomes caution.

When the mushrooms are eaten, they get their kind of revenge. They eat you, in a way. The humans slowly start turning into jumbo-sized mushrooms themselves. Previously, the group discovered another wrecked yacht on the island, but no sign of the passengers. Later on, these castaways figure out the previous castaways have joined the fungus club.

The last part of the film really gets surreal as we see the half humans and the full fledged mushroom people mixing together and having a good time. The soundtrack is super creepy with the mushroom people's croaking voices echoing through the forest.

Instead of the "final girl" surviving as in a lot of horror flicks, in this one, a man survives. Well, sort of. He's been relating the tale to us at the opening of the movie, but we never see his face. At the end of the movie, he turns around and confesses that he could stand it no longer and he ate the mushrooms. We now see his fungi face and know he's headed into mushroom land.

The original title, Matango, was changed to Attack of the Mushroom People after American International picked up the film to distribute to television. There was supposedly a negative reaction in Japan to the movie, as the actors in the semi-human stage resembled victims of Hiroshima.

A departure from Godzilla and its progeny, the movie is a must-see for fans of truly fantastic cinema.

ISLAND OF LOST SOULS

Without a doubt, this is one of the great horror classics of early cinema. The novel it is derived from, The Island of Dr. Moreau by H.G. Wells, is my favorite Wells novel. The first time I read the novel, it was deeply weird and unsettling, but the movie is even more so! Maybe that's why Wells didn't like the movie; it went too far.

It certainly is lurid enough. A pre-code film, it could get away with a lot of things they wouldn't be able to do just a few years hence. But that's what makes it so powerful, eerie, and thrilling.

Charles Laughton is brilliant as the twisted Dr. Moreau. In his white suit, coupled with his satanic-like beard and mustache, he struts his way through the movie as though he is a god. Why not? He sees himself as one and he even says so in the film. In the novel, it seemed like Moreau was experimenting with the plasticity of animal flesh, trying through surgery to form them into human-like creatures. Darwinism was in full swing during the time of the novel, and Wells was perhaps, zinging the evolutionist theory. I also took it as an anti-vivisectionist argument.

The only human beings on the island at first, are a castaway, Parker, (Richard Arlen), Dr. Moreau, and Montgomery, (Arthur Hohl). Parker's fiancé, Ruth, (Leila Hyams), along with Captain Donahue, are busy tracking down Parker to Moreau's island.

At first, Parker mistakenly thinks Moreau is vivisecting animals. Their screams prompt him to run away. As he makes his way through the jungle, he runs into a vast assortment of beast people which baffle him. Moreau, however, catches up with Parker, and he cracks his whip to make the beast people recite the law. If you wonder where Devo ever got the phrase, *Are We Not Men?* it is both from the novel and the movie.

The Sayer of the Law is an almost unrecognizable Bela Lugosi. His face is completely covered with hair, and only his distinctive voice lets you know who he is. You could say that Lugosi played a Wolf Man before Lon Chaney did. His mournful voice fits perfectly with the pathetic recital of the cruel laws.

Moreau shows Parker around his House of Pain, where a

suffering manimal lies moaning in agony. Moreau's callous disregard for the pain he inflicts is infuriating. He is a true sociopath.

Meanwhile, in a great departure from the novel, Moreau has surgically transformed a panther into a beautiful, young woman named Lota. Moreau, perverted little devil that he is, is excited to see if Parker is attracted to Lota, and hopes that they "mate." Parker, who already knows that Moreau is transforming animals into humans, doesn't suspect Lota is one of Moreau's experiments. When he does find out, Moreau gets knocked on his keister by the enraged Parker.

Ruth and Captain Donahue find the island and plan to take Parker away. Moreau talks them into staying the night. Big mistake.

Moreau whispers deadly orders to one of the most bestial of the Beast folk, Ouran. Although we don't know what he says, it's pretty evident that Ouran is to break into Ruth's room to commit a vile act. Fortunately, she screams and frightens Ouran away.

Captain Donahue is knocked off by Ouran at Moreau's orders. Ouran goes to the Sayer of the Law to tell him that Moreau told him to break the law and spill blood, so the furry Sayer reasons that Moreau can also die. Say no more!

In a scene out of anyone's nightmare, the Beast folk burn down their huts and converge on Moreau's House of Pain, to put a whole lot of hurt on Moreau. As they march toward the camera, we get to see the incredible makeup jobs that were worn by the actors, still unsettling even by today's standards.

The Beast people hold Moreau down on his operating table, break the glass containers where the surgical instruments are contained, and they start to do their own kind of surgery on Moreau.

Although we never see anything, as the Beast people huddle around him, Laughton's screams of agony send a chill up the spine.

Special mention should be made of Kathleen Burke, who plays Lota. Probably her most famous role, it's also her first one, and she plays Lota with a sweet, childlike demeanor. Her movements are quick and graceful as the panther she is made from. Her other biggest genre role is as Lionel Atwill's short-lived wife, in Murders at the Zoo.

In all, though, this is Laughton's show, and I really can't imagine any other actor playing the role better than he. His face glows with maniacal pride as he listens to the Beast folk drone out his laws. It's a chilling reminder that a few years down the road, another madman would lead his minions to destruction in Europe.

RETURN OF THE VAMPIRE

I love this movie. There, I said it. To me, it's a high point in Lugosi's career. He is more or less Dracula under another name, and he plays it to the hilt.

A Columbia B picture it may be, but it positively oozes with atmosphere. Also, a good supporting cast made this movie rise above its lower status.

Lugosi is Armand Tesla, a vampire who gets knocked off when the movie begins, but during the London blitz in WW II, his cemetery bedroom is blown up by the nasty Nazis. A couple of gravediggers who are putting back bodies that have been uprooted, find Tesla's body with a spike through his chest. One of them thoughtfully removes it and that's all Tesla needed to make a return to the land of the living.

We have a female Van Helsing type named Lady Jane Ainsley in this go-around, played by Freida Inescort. She helped put out Tesla's lights the first time around, and she's still there twenty years later to have another whack at it. Her assistant at her clinic, Andreas, (Matt Willis), was a slave to Tesla way back when, but he was no ordinary servant, he was a werewolf! Sort of a hairy Renfield.

Of course, like all good vampires, he wants to get even with Lady Jane Ainsley for sending him to skeleton city. He strikes back at her by attacking her son's fiancé, Nikki Saunders, (Nina Foch).

Nikki also happens to be the daughter of Professor Saunders, who we saw in the opening of the movie. He was the instigator that put Tesla out of commission, while Lady Jane assisted.

Tesla tries his best to ruin everybody's day, but he didn't reckon on Andreas getting religion. After Andreas is shot by the police, he tries to get his master to help him, but as far as Tesla is concerned, easy come, easy go. Tesla had kidnapped Nikki and brought her back to his tomb. Andreas, who was told to go to the corner to die, espies a small crucifix in the dirt of the churchyard. Andreas transforms back into a man and uses the crucifix to force Tesla into the sunlight. After Tesla falls to the ground, Andreas makes sure Tesla is a goner by driving another spike through his heart. I wonder if the previous hole was still there to use as a guide.

There is a lot to recommend about this movie. First off, it's a whole lot of fun, and it's never boring. As for the cast, this is Lugosi's show and he knows it. The first time we see him in the graveyard wearing his Dracula-like black cape is a standout scene. I remember that particular scene was featured at the beginning of the TV documentary series, Hollywood and the Stars. The episode was titled Monsters We Have Known and Loved. I had not seen Return of the Vampire at that point, and I thought there was a Dracula movie I didn't know about. It took me years to finally catch this movie on the tube. Seeing Lugosi in this movie gives you a good idea of how he would have looked if he got to play Dracula in the two *House Of* movies. Oh well, what's done is done.

Matt Willis, in the biggest role of his career, makes a sympathetic slave as Andreas. His mental torment while he's in human form, which transforms into his gleeful servitude shows that Willis had a lot of range he never got to use elsewhere. Another great scene is when two cops try to nab him while he's in human form. As they struggle with him, he turns into his werewolf self. The werewolf makeup is very similar to Columbia's later film, The Werewolf. People have remarked that he looks more like a dog, but hey, wolves and dogs are canines. Makes sense to me.

Frieda Inescort and Nina Foch both play their roles well, and it particularly refreshing in an old movie to have a middle-aged woman be the protagonist. If there's any misstep at all, it's in the end. Actor Miles Mander breaks the fourth wall to ask the audience if we believe in vampires. That would play in a comedy, but it's the same type of unnecessary levity that spoiled the ending of The Beast with Five Fingers.

Tesla's demise is also startling for the era. We see his face melt off his skull in closeup. Evidently they made a wax Lugosi face and heated it to melt. It's very effective.

I love this movie. Did I already say that?

THE FLY PAPERS

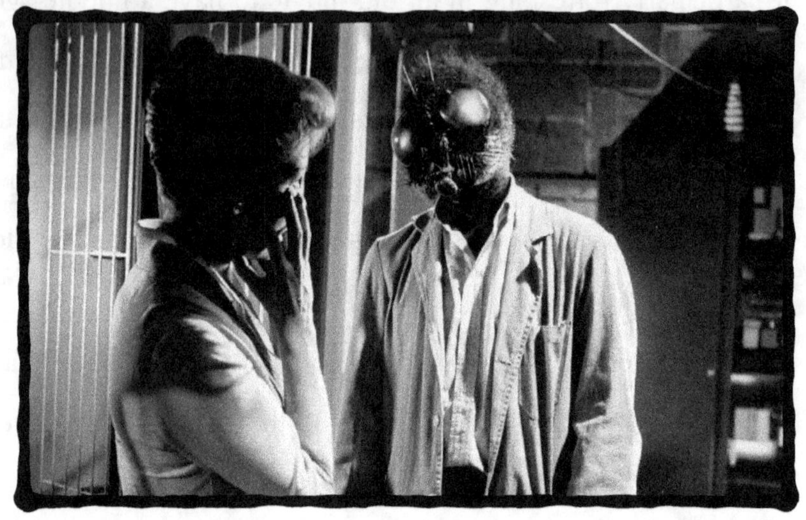

One of my earliest childhood memories is going to see this movie as a small child, sitting in the front seat of my parent's car at the drive-in. Just as the credits start, with a buzzing sound and a fly crawling on a mesh screen, I fell asleep. I had it described to me the next day, and I felt I had missed a whopper of a movie. I didn't get to see it until it appeared on TV.

Vincent Price is the star, and most people at the time would have expected villainy from him. But no, he's the closest thing to a hero in this film. The fly guy is future Voyage to the Bottom of the Sea star, "Al" Hedison, later to be rechristened "David."

The film is based on a short story by George Langelaan, a French writer and journalist. Andre Delambre, (Hedison), invents the disintegrator-integrator machine, capable of breaking down matter and transporting it to another location. His faithful wife, Helene, (Patricia Owens), winds up as a murder suspect when at the beginning of the film, Andre's body is partially hanging out of a hydraulic press. His head and arm are flat as a pancake, but they can still identify the body by a scar on his leg. Helene confesses that she did it and baffles both Andre's brother, Francois, (Price), and the police Inspector Charas, played by Herbert Marshall.

Long story short, Andre tried the machine on himself but didn't know he had a fly hitchhiking in the booth with him. For most of the film his head is draped in a black cloth and he keeps his fly arm tucked in his pocket. Helene is the only one that knows he's a fly guy. Their only hope is to find the fly that is buzzing around which is sporting his human head and arm. Helene and her son almost catch the little bugger but he gets away into the garden. At a loss of what to do, Helene persuades Andre to go through his atomic mixmaster again and maybe come out a little less buggy. He doesn't, and we are treated to the sight of Andre's fly head. After Andre trashes the place, he asks Helene to help him commit suicide by having his fly parts squished in their factory.

Francois had earlier fibbed to Helene that he had found the white-headed fly, but he wouldn't destroy it unless Helene spilled the beans. After she did, Francois and the inspector go

outside and we now have one of the most iconic lines in moviedom ring in our ears. "Help me! Help me!" The duo finds the Andre fly trapped in a web about to be gobbled up by a spider. Once again, Andre is flattened to death, this time by a rock.

The Fly has been described by critics as lurid, ridiculous, shocking, original, and creepy as hell. It is hard not to laugh at the fly in the web scene, as Price and Marshall did while shooting it. At the same time, the high-pitched voice coupled with a heavily made-up Hedison is chilling.

The picture is handsomely mounted in glorious color, unlike many of the B-movies of the 50s. Being a cat lover, I hate the scene where the family cat is used in a failed experiment, although Andre thought the cat would be safe. In the original story, when Andre goes through a second time, he's not just fly parts, he's also cat parts, which would have been a truly grotesque sight.

Another highlight of the film is when Helene pulls the cloth off of Andre's head and screams. We cut to a fly-eye view of dozens of Helene's screaming in horror. It is also not without pathos. After Andre destroys his lab and right before he goes to get squashed, he writes on the blackboard "Love you" for Helene, his fly arm trying to keep his human arm from demonstrating such affections.

Price has not much to do except pop in and out, pretty much standing in for the audience to find out what's what. He was more prominent in the sequel, Return of the Fly.

In Return of the Fly, we find ourselves in a black and white world, where Andre's son, Philippe, is attending his mother's funeral. Francois, (Vincent Price), takes Philippe to the lab where his father went all buggy. They were able to use the standing set from the first movie, so you can see where Andre had written "love you" on the chalkboard.

Of course, Philippe wants to follow in his father's fly steps, but unfortunately for him, his assistant, Ronald, (David Frankham), is a scoundrel in disguise, on the run from British authorities. Ronald sees big bucks coming his way from stealing the plans for the disintegrator-integrator, now that Philipe has picked up where his father left off. A British agent confronts Ronald in the lab while he's busy in skullduggery. Ronald knocks out the Brit, and throws him into the D-I machine to make him disappear temporarily. When Ronald re-integrates the agent, he's in for a big surprise. Earlier, Philipe had been testing a rat which he sent out into the ether but hadn't brought him back yet. Now the Brit and the rat's atoms are mixed up and we have a pretty grisly sight.

So we knew Philipe wouldn't get through the movie without a round trip in the D-I machine, so when Ronald is exposed for the crook he is, a fight ensues with Philippe getting the worst of it. Ronald throws him into the machine and just for laughs, throws a fly in with him. Zap! Philipe gone!

Francois returns to the lab and turns on the mixmaster machine. You guessed it. Philipe has a fly head and arm and he's buzzing mad. After knocking off a couple of bad guys, the little fly man is caught and Philipe is run through the machine again and comes out fine and dandy. Even the fly came out well.

The film was made in a hurry to cash in on the success of the first film. Price has said that he thought the original script was better than the first film, but a lot of it got lost in translation, I guess. It was shot in black and white Cinemascope, though, which gives it some class. It comes across as what it is, a B movie quickly made. Even though the fly head on Philipe is more accurate, the mistake for me is that they made it so damn big. If it had been made smaller it would have been more effective. This way it seems like the fly guy would have trouble just walking into a room.

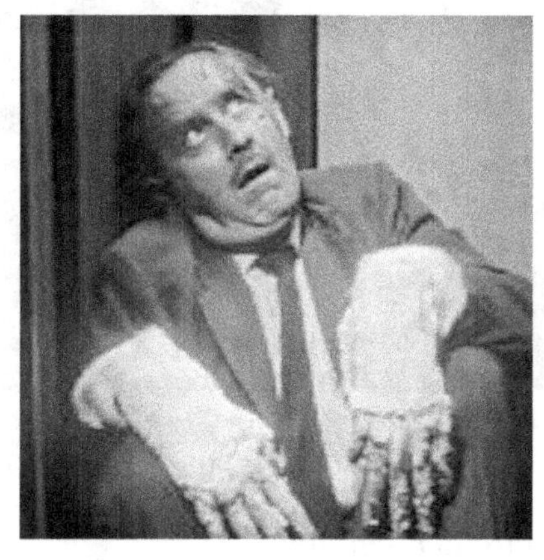

When I was a kid and saw this in the theater I was freaked out by the guy who got mixed up with the rat. His rat hands and feet and the expression on his face gave me the willies. The fly itself didn't scare me, though, but the scene of the rat with tiny human hands is a sick sight.

The Curse of the Fly usually gets dismissed, but I found it very entertaining. The writers got kind of lost in the family tree, since the older Delambre, played by Brian Donlevy, by rights should be Philipe as an old man, but instead is named Henri.

They are still futzing around with the teleporter, but are no better at it than the previous family members. Henri has two sons, Martin and Albert. Martin has problems, though. He has recessive fly genes which make him age rapidly unless he keeps taking a serum. Albert, who stays at their lab in London, really wants nothing to do with this crazy stuff.

Martin meets Patricia, who we saw at the beginning of the film escaping from an insane asylum. They fall in love, not knowing each other's secrets.

The Delambres keep their previous misfired misfits locked up on the grounds. We get a peek at them sometimes, especially Martin's

first wife, who can get into the house and play the piano. Of course, half her face looks like a melted candle.

The police track Patricia to the Delambre house, and when the current inspector consults with an aging Inspector Charas from the first movie, they find out about the wacky Delambre family and their failed experiments.

When Henri knows the jig is up, he decides to dispose of the creatures they created by sending them off to Albert in London. We then have the big shock scene of this movie. The monstrosities are fused together during integration and look like a wobbly mass of flesh. Albert gets an ax and puts them out of their misery. In a frenzy, he also wrecks the integration machine.

Henri wants Martin and Patricia to zap themselves to London with Albert to beat the cops as they close in. Henri goes first, but surprise! The integration machine is wrecked so Henri is reduced to cosmic dust. Patricia was supposed to be next, but her hubby,

Martin didn't get his serum in time, so he does a Dorian Gray and dies. The police rescue Patricia, if you can call going back to the madhouse a rescue.

It sounds convoluted, but watching it is like experiencing someone's nightmare. Director Don Sharpe, who also directed two great horror films, Kiss of the Vampire and Witchcraft, does a nice job with the atmosphere and keeps it moving. One misstep is having one of the Asian housekeepers played by an obvious Caucasian woman with bad makeup. Having her husband played by the real deal, Burt Kwouk, just magnifies the problem. So many Asian actresses they could have gotten, why did they do that?

STRANGER ON THE THIRD FLOOR

I remember the first time I saw this little gem on a UHF station one afternoon. I thought I knew most of Peter Lorre's films, but this early film noir horror flick combo took me by surprise.

The thing I like about B-movies is their brevity. Nowadays, it seems every movie is bloated out to run 2-3 hours. You can watch a B-movie for an hour and change.

Although Lorre is the star, he says very little, and you mostly see him skulking around in the shadows of a boarding house. The hero of the piece is John McGuire, and this movie is the highlight of an otherwise lackluster career.

In the film, his character is supposedly a witness to a murder committed in a diner. The wrong guy is pegged for it, though, and it's none other than poor Elisha Cook. McGuire's finance, played by Margaret Tallichet, thinks they may have arrested the wrong man. Meanwhile, an obnoxious neighbor, played by professional pain in the ass Charles Halton, makes McGuire's life miserable by constantly complaining to anyone who will listen.

Lorre is spotted periodically, going in and out of the building, and always wearing a long scarf. McGuire is suspicious of this furtive figure hanging around, and when the neighbor is murdered, McGuire believes the stranger is the killer and not Cook.

The film's highlight is a cool dream sequence, presenting a montage of distorted angles, black shadows crisscrossing the scenes, and the added punch of Lorre invading the dream. It also makes use of the interior monologue of the protagonist, as the audience hears what the person is thinking, a method which would be utilized much more in the Inner Sanctum series of movies.

It's Tallichet's character who winds up the film when she spots Lorre feeding a dog on the street. She talks to him and it's quickly pretty clear that Lorre is off his trolley. He's an escapee from the booby hatch and he doesn't want to go back. Thinking the woman is going to take him back there, she tries to get away from him, but as they struggle in the street, the madman is hit by a truck. He dies happy though. He doesn't have to go back to the asylum.

Typically for the time period, the critics pretty much dismissed the film as unoriginal or with too much German influence, or whatever their sourpuss minds could think of. Time, however, is the true arbiter of what leaves a lasting impression on the public, and I think anyone who sees this little B will not forget it.

VILLAGE OF THE DAMNED

It occurs to me that you could make a horror movie out of anything if you just put "of the Damned" after it. Laundromat of the Damned, Parking Garage of the Damned, Pizza of the Damned, Doggies of the Damned, etc. But I digress.

For my money, Village of the Damned is one of the classic science fiction films of the 50s-60s era. Based on John Wyndham's book The Midwich Cuckoos, it tells the tale of a long-distance alien invasion by ingenious means. In the film, where these creepy kids came from is left vague, but it hints that they are alien seeds, that were zapped through outer space. In different parts of the world, women of childbearing age suddenly find themselves pregnant. The children produced are emotionless, blonde-haired kids whose eyes glow on command when they want to bump off somebody. They don't do the actual killing, they make people kill themselves.

The film stars George Sanders, in a late in-his-career starring role. Barbara Shelley plays the wife who is one of the women who finds herself carrying an unknown bundle of joy.

The movie is a marvel of low key theatrics, with practically no special effects, other than the children's eyes glowing. Martin Stevens plays the main child, David, the "son" of George Sanders.

Although his voice is dubbed, his manner and facial expressions are excellently portrayed, and he is one spooky kid. Sanders gets to show a heroic side, quite different from the usual snide portrayals he was accustomed to. He acquits himself remarkably well, underplaying just enough to be believable. Shelley is touching as the mother, who tries to get through to her cold, aloof son. Michael Gwynn, as Sander's brother, gives a solid performance as the army officer who tries to warn Sanders that the children are evil.

After the children have killed off one too many people and nearly killed Sanders's brother, he decides he must destroy them before they proliferate, as they have already threatened to do.

I won't give away the ending on this one, because I don't think it gets much airplay, and I think you should seek it out for yourself. You also might want to see the follow-up, Children of the Damned. Not a sequel, but a different take on the story.

FRANKENSTEIN 1970

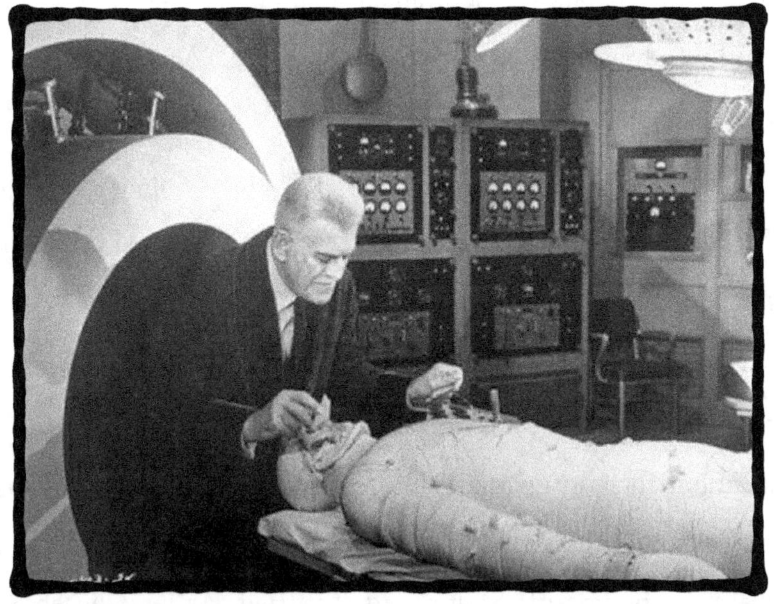

This much-maligned film is one I'm very fond of. I don't quite know why, but I'll use this essay as talk therapy to find out why.

I know all the brickbats thrown at it. The great opening sequence, no real monster, Karloff is hammy, the wrapped-up monster looks like he's wearing a bucket on his head, etc. I agree with all that, but I like the movie despite it.

Karloff gets to play an actual Frankenstein in this one. Of course, Boris couldn't get away with just looking normal, so he's scarred and disfigured from his being tortured in a Nazi prison camp. Karloff needs money, so against his better judgment, he lets a TV crew inside his castle to make a documentary. The wonderful first scene is actually the film crew shooting part of their documentary on the Frankenstein family. The crew is led by the loud, brash, Mr. Rowe, played by Red Barry. We also have crew members Mike, Judy, and Carolyn.

In the Baron's household are his butler, Shuter, his close friend, Gottfried, and Hans, a big galoot who played the monster in the opener.

Much like Peter Cushing in Hammer Film's Frankenstein and the Monster from Hell, the Baron sees that he doesn't have to send out for body parts when he has potential donors under his roof, namely the movie people he detests. When he runs out of them, he bumps off Shuter and Gottfried. At least he shows a little remorse when he kills the last two. He brings the monster to life before it has all its working parts, but the monster has the uncanny ability to locate people even when he has no eyes.

The Baron's big mistake was putting his butler's brain into the monster, who turns on him in his lab. They are killed by radioactive steam spewing out of the Baron's atomic reactor. The big anti-climax is when the monster's face is unmasked at the end, and it's Karloff's normal face, looking like he should be introducing a new episode of Thriller.

My fondness for this movie is partly nostalgia. I saw it in the theater when I was around 6 years old, but I knew who Karloff was and I knew how the Frankenstein monster was supposed to look. I was very disappointed at the ending. I didn't see it again until it started showing up on TV, and the more times I watched it, the more I enjoyed it. While critics may say Karloff is hammy in it, I think that's part of the fun. It would be quite deadly if he played it straight. It looks nice in its original widescreen, and of course, I love that it's in black and white. Everyone loves the opening scene, and yeah, we all wish that the rest of the movie was like that, but once you know it isn't you can start to enjoy it anyway.

A comic highlight is when the Baron accidentally drops some severed eyeballs on the floor. His reaction is priceless; *oh great, what else can go wrong?* When he disposes of the ruined peepers in his garbage disposal the sound is…well, as it's been pointed out elsewhere, it sounds like a toilet flushing.

The monster freely roaming around without eyes is so goofy you just have to laugh at his navigation skills. It's like Helen Keller's teacher, Annie Sullivan had been tutoring the monster in his downtime. I wish he didn't knock off Judy so soon. Charlotte Austin, who plays Judy, is not just a good actor, but she's sexy as well. Rudolph Anders, who plays Gottfried, knows how to chew the scenery, as we saw in She Demons, but here he is playing straight, so Karloff can have all the fun.

I think the only reason the wrapped monster looks like he has a big bucket over his head, is because they wanted the audience to think they'll eventually see the famous "square-headed" monster before it's over. Wrong.

Maybe I can't explain why I love this movie. I just do. It's fun and silly and Karloff is having a good time. If Vincent Price can ham it up in Pit and the Pendulum, then let Karloff have this one.

THE THINGS

John W. Campbell's novella, "Who Goes There?" is considered one of the classics of science fiction literature. It spawned two movies with similar titles but very different approaches. Both films are, for me anyway, classics in the genre.

Howard Hawks, the producer of The Thing from Another World, and who certainly affected the direction of Christian Nyby, took a road not taken for him. It's his only science fiction film, and it is a doozy.

1950 was an early start in the science fiction movie race that became more and more prevalent as the decade rolled on. Most of them were B movies and featured cheap effects, some successful, some not. But The Thing from Another World was not a low-budget knockoff. Its special effects were practically nil, and the cast included no major stars. But the Hawks' trademark of rapid, overlapping dialogue and realistic characterizations, gave the movie a non-stop momentum that has seldom been equaled. So many modern films have a bloated running time. I bet Hawks would cut their running time in half.

Campbell's story has a shape-shifting alien, which would have been pretty difficult to do with that decade's state-of-the-art special effects. The aspect of the alien taking over the shape of its human victim would be easy enough, but showing the alien in its true form would be problematic. I think the best bet would have been a stop-motion alien animated by Ray Harryhausen, but the powers that be decided to go with a much simpler approach.

The movie doesn't share much with the original story. It keeps the plot line of an alien spacecraft that crash landed in the frigid north and the discovery of the frozen body of an alien. They inadvertently blow up the ship with explosives, but the alien can be cut out of the ice and transferred to the base.

Instead of a shape-shifting alien, we have a combination Frankenstein/Dracula monster in the person of James Arness. Never do we get a good look at the monster, but in still photos, we can see he was basically a dome-headed, dark-eyed alien with razor-sharp claws. After the thing is thawed out and starts killing sled dogs, the men are frightened to learn that the monster lives on blood. The scientist at the base, Dr. Carrington, reveals that the alien is evolved from plant life. Scotty, the news reporter on

the scene amusingly says, "An intellectual carrot? The mind boggles." Carrington, as we discover, is on the creature's side, and wants to communicate with it. When one of the Thing's arms is torn off by a sled dog, Carrington takes seeds from it and starts growing new aliens.

Eventually, the Thing is electrocuted to death and ends up as a smoking salad on the floor. The film's most immortal line is at the end. *Keep watching the skies!*

Kenneth Tobey as Hendry is the main character, although I see it more as an ensemble cast since so many of them have important parts to play. Even the token female, Nikki, is the one who comes up with the way to kill the thing.

All in all, even though it's only loosely based on the story, this "thing" is one of the best science fiction films of all time.

John Carpenter's version of The Thing was not well received in its time, but has since become a cult favorite. Reviews at the time condemned its gore and extreme special effects. Nowadays such things are par for the course. This version is not a remake of the 50s version. This film sticks very close to Campbell's original story about a shape shifting alien. With a mixture of puppetry, prosthetics, and animatronics, this thing is very formidable indeed.

As in the story, paranoia reigns. The alien gets taken to the base and thawed out. It starts by mimicking the sled dogs, and from there moves on to the people. Since even pieces of the thing can stay alive and consume a new victim, nobody is safe from the thing or each other. Kurt Russell plays MacReady, the nominal lead in the film, although it is more like an ensemble as was the previous version.

The most spectacular special effects sequence to me is when Norris, one of the men, has a heart attack, and he is laid on a table so Dr. Copper can try to save his life. Unfortunately, Norris is not a man at all; he is part of the thing, and as Dr. Copper tries to defibrillate the man's chest, it opens up into a sharp-toothed mouth that bites the doctor's hands off. As everyone goes crazy at this point, MacReady burns Norris's body up with a flame thrower. But Norris's head detaches and falls on the floor. Then, with the head upside down, it sprouts insect-like legs and attempts to escape. It's an image out of a nightmare.

It took me a few viewings, but I got to like this film, as time has taken away all the shock value of the effects. The acting is top-notch, and since you don't know who will survive, the suspense is always present. Unlike the 50s version, the film ends on a downbeat note, as the two survivors, MacReady and Childs, watch their camp burn to the ground, having trapped the thing inside to kill it once and for all. Whether the two men will freeze to death or not, is up in the air.

DIE, MONSTER, DIE

Here we have another attempt to make a movie from a Lovecraft story. The story this time is one of Lovecraft's best, The Colour Out of Space.

AIP had three tries at Lovecraft. The Haunted Palace, The Dunwich Horror, and this one. Oddly enough, the one that was masquerading as a Poe story, The Haunted Palace, is the one I consider the best of the three. I think Die, Monster Die edges out The Dunwich Horror as the better film in my estimation. Dunwich Horror is very hard to adapt, and AIP took the easy way out by making Wilbur Whateley a normal-looking 70s-era guy instead of the half-human character from the story. Trying to depict one of Lovecraft's Old Ones, was also beyond the capabilities of AIP's special effects department.

Die Monster, Die doesn't have to depend on special effects to tell the story, although it does have several memorable sequences.

The big plus for this movie is the stars: Boris Karloff and Nick Adams. The town of Arkham, which in the story is in New England, is transferred to Great Britain. Adams seems out of place in this fictional English town, but that's the point. He's a city guy and not used to unfriendly villagers.

Adams's character, Stephen Reinhart, is there to look for his fiancé, Susan Whitley, (Suzan Farmer). He is given a cold reception from the townspeople when he seeks transportation to the Whitley mansion. Things don't get any better when he makes it to the estate, and Nahum Whitley, (Karloff), tells him to get lost. Susan's mother, who is bedridden and hidden behind a veil over the bed, is more sympathetic and wants Stephen to get her daughter the heck out of there.

The upshot is that a meteor hit the land years ago, and produced healthy growths of foliage in barren soil. Nahum took the meteorite and put it in his basement, and had been experimenting with the radioactivity emanating from it. Unfortunately, his experiments affected his wife, who is physically decaying by the day, and even the family butler drops dead from exposure while the family is eating dinner. In a particularly creepy scene, Stephen and Susan break into a hothouse on the grounds and find all kinds of weird-looking, mutated animals in cages. Stephen comments, "it's like a zoo in Hell." I think that would be a good tourist attraction myself.

After Letitia, the wife, takes the express train to ugly city and dissolves into mush, Nahum decides he's had it with the meteorite and he takes an ax to it. Not a good idea. He gets infected quickly by the rays and turns into a bullet-headed, green, glowing monster. We have a lot of action now with the two people trying to keep away from Mr. Glow Guy. But he finally falls off a balcony and breaks up into pieces. (A similar death met Karloff in The Invisible Ray).

The movie is not long enough to wear out its welcome, and even though we know it's not Karloff playing the monster at the end, the monster's face resembles Karloff, so that'll have to do.

Daniel Haller directed this one, and although he doesn't do a bad job, it does make you wonder how Roger Corman would have handled it. But it's great to see Karloff in one of his last meaty roles. Targets would be the only notable role left for him. The Mexican quickies he did are hardly worth mentioning.

ABBOTT AND COSTELLO MEET THE MUMMY

This movie marks the duo's last feature at Universal-International, and the last time they would meet any monsters. This one tends to get placed at the bottom of the monster's list, but I like it better than The Invisible Man and the Jekyll and Hyde movies.

It might be my fondness for living mummies, or that it's the last time we'll see the boys in a Universal movie. Their next movie is their last one, the dismal Dance with Me, Henry.

The supporting players are a fun bunch. For the baddies, we have Michael Ansara, Marie Windsor, Richard Deacon, and Mel Welles. A special note is that the mummy is played by stuntman Eddie Parker, who stood in for Lugosi in Frankenstein Meets the Wolfman and then donned the Mr. Hyde disguise when A & C met him. The mummy makeup isn't as good as Chaney's in his mummy flicks, but I don't think it matters at this point.

The boys try to get a job with Professor Zoomer, who is transporting the mummy Klaris to America. How Kharis became Klaris is never explained. Maybe he was in the witness protection program. Klaris wears a medallion that is a map to a hidden treasure. Semu, (Richard Deacon), is the head of the cult of Klaris, and he wants the mummy to stay put so they can get the medallion and find the treasure.

I won't go into detail but all sorts of shenanigans take place, and the boys get to do some burlesque routines along the way, most notably when they are ordered to dig a hole with either a pick or a shovel. All Abbott has to say to Costello is "take your pick" to start an argument.

One cockeyed aspect of the movie is that Semu intended to kill Bud and Lou, and his henchmen had earlier killed Professor Zoomer. But at the end of the movie, when Klaris is destroyed in an explosion, the blast reveals the treasure. Then Bud and Lou get chummy with Semu and convince him to open up a nightclub with the money. Talk about letting bygones be bygones.

THE H-MAN

When I saw this movie in the theater, they had one of those giveaways that studios would use to promote a particular movie. Kind of like a toy surprise in Cracker Jacks. For this movie, you were given a flat dried-out sponge shaped like a human. Drop it in water and the sponge absorbed it and expanded. Not much like what the H-Men in the movie do, but it was still kind of neat. One of the many things I wish I still had.

Ishiro Hondo, the director of many Godzilla movies, takes on this gangster/science fiction story with mixed results. The gangster aspect has to do with drug dealers and the science fiction part is the H-Men. Once again, radioactivity is the cause that creates the title creatures. They can appear as a shimmering human outline, or just be a blobby mess that can creep around and nab victims. When an H-Man gets ahold of you, it's dinnertime and it dissolves you, leaving your clothes behind. There are several unsettling times we see the H-Man at work, as the human victims seem to deflate before our eyes. That scared me as a kid. The best scene is a flashback when we see a derelict ship where the H-Men are the "crew."

On the minus side, I thought too much time is spent on the crime story and not enough on the H-Men. Maybe they thought the storyline of the H-Men alone wouldn't fill out a movie. It's certainly a different type of Japanese thriller, and it's enhanced by being shot in color. The fiery death of the H-Men in the town sewers is another highlight.

Like a lot of Japanese movies of the time, there was an American version and the original Japanese version. When I was a kid I saw the American version. I prefer it because it's shorter than the Japanese version. Some of the gangster element was edited out, making it a tighter movie. Both versions are on the DVDs currently available.

HORROR OF PARTY BEACH

The kids of my generation were first made aware of this film courtesy of a Famous Monster's special issue promo. The story was told in photos, some surprisingly gory shots for the time. Another item I owned and lost.

I finally saw it on TV and didn't know what to make of it at first. I got a kick out of the fact that it was filmed in New England, Connecticut to be exact. Practically my backyard. For the mid-60s the gore was surprising and unsettling, especially juxtaposed with the silly beach party scenes.

The monsters are rather unique. Their lizard-like heads house a mouth that seems to be stuffed with hot dogs. Their claws certainly do the dirty work when we see a beach girl, females at a pajama party, and assorted townspeople get sliced up real good. Plus, I always felt that blood looks worse in black and white.

I think in later years, Del Tenney claimed it was purposely campy, and maybe he did mean it that way. The movie certainly comes off that way. What's particularly egregious is the black maid, Eulabelle, who acts like she came out of an old forties movie instead of the more enlightened 60s. I suppose you could say they were sending up that stereotype, but it's still pretty painful to watch nowadays.

The monsters are a hoot, and if you look at it as a tongue-in-cheek enterprise, it is very entertaining. Oh, the rock band, The Del Aires, are quite good.

FREAKS

Although released in the early 1930s, this movie is still controversial for its use of genuine human oddities instead of actors in elaborate makeup. The first time I became aware of it was in an old Castle of Frankenstein issue that featured an article on it. A photo of the armless and legless Prince Randian was a little gut-wrenching to my young eyes. The problem was trying to see the film during the 60s. It was never released to television, being considered too strong for the couch crowd.

I finally got to see it in a revival house in Boston, and my first viewing rather stunned me. However, like many contemporary film critics, I came to view the film as a mostly sympathetic story.

Although some of the sideshow participants rather regretted appearing in it, most of them seemed to have enjoyed the prospect of sharing their mostly true selves to the world. You can't help but admire how people without arms can use their feet as a substitute, that conjoined twins are just as human as anyone else, that little people can go through life with dignity, and amazingly, that an armless and legless man can roll and light a cigarette!

Harry Earles, the midget that is the lead of the story, was the one who suggested to director Tod Browning that they make a movie of a short story, Spurs. The story is remarkably similar to the screenplay, both involving a conniving female circus performer who marries Jacques, a midget with the circus. He has inherited a lot of money so she figures he'll die soon and she'll have everything. In the story she gets drunk and humiliates Jacques by picking him up and putting him on her shoulders, saying she could carry the "little ape" across France and back. Jacques's revenge in the story is different from the movie, which is where the film earns the title, horror film.

In the film, Cleopatra, and her lover, Hercules, the strongman, are the plotters. Hans, (Harry Earles), is inheriting a fortune, so Cleopatra gets him to marry her, with the intent of poisoning him and getting all the money. When the plot fails, the "freaks" band together and take their revenge on the two would-be murderers. The ending was so disturbing that one of the scenes was omitted. Originally, Hercules was to be castrated and would be shown later in the circus singing soprano. Kind of horrifying and funny at the same time. But Cleopatra's fate we do see, as she astonishingly has been transformed into a human chicken, her feathered lower torso is legless, her face scarred and deformed, a squawking monstrosity.

For me, the most horrific scene is at the climax when during a storm, the freaks pursue Cleopatra. We see some of them brandishing knives, while others, like the "pinheads" and Prince Randian, with a knife in his mouth, are crawling through the mud under the circus wagon. How Randian could do any harm in his condition is left for us to wonder.

The film was too much for Depression-era audiences and quickly bombed. It was later sold to exploitation operators where it circulated for decades. Now, it is an established cult film and has been included in the National Film Registry. Famed cartoonist Bill Griffith was inspired to create his character Zippy the Pinhead after he caught the film in the early 60s. In Freaks, one of the first real-life oddities we see is Schlitzie, a microcephalic male dressed as a female.

Despite its age, it is not for the squeamish. Be warned.

THE HUMAN DUPLICATORS

Here's a perfect drive-in movie. Low budget but colorful flick, with aliens, government agents, and a raft of familiar character actors.

King-sized Richard Kiel plays Kolos, an alien whose mission is to duplicate Earthlings to take over the planet. I imagine that would take some time if they do it one by one. Dr. Dornheimer is already working on making androids, so Kolos horns in on the project by duplicating Dr. Dornheimer and tossing the real guy into a cell. Then Kolos starts his plan of world conquest.

Meanwhile, agents of the NIA, the national intelligence agency, are on the case. Glenn Martin sneaks into the lab, but

Kolos ruins his plans by abducting him and then duplicating him. The real Glenn joins the real Dornheimer in his cell. At least they have something in common to talk about.

Fake Glenn is suspected of not being the real deal by his girlfriend, Gale, who is not used to Glenn being such a cold fish.

Fake Glenn breaks into a high security area to steal electronics of some sort. Gale has followed him, along with some cops, who shoot up Glenn as he's leaving. Fake Glenn's arm gets stuck in a door, but since he can always get another one, he leaves it behind.

Dornheimer's daughter, Lisa, has been left free to run around by Kolos, who's gone soft on her. She goes to where her father and Glenn are and gives Glenn his handy dandy secret agent coin that contains a wire/saw. Dornheimer tells Glenn that the dupes can be zapped out of commission by the laser pulse ray in the lab.

Lisa is supposed to be next on the list to duplicate, but Kolos is not having it. Dornheimer/dupe proclaims himself the new leader of the invasion. Fake Glenn is still loyal to Kolos so the two dupes fight and kill each other. Kolos has failed in his mission and now has to return to his home planet to be destroyed. Somebody should have given Kolos some brochures of South America, instead.

It sounds confusing, but it's not really. It's goofy and fun, and the cast is what makes it so. Aside from Kiel, we have in the lead, George Nader of Robot Monster fame, which I suppose makes this movie a step up for him. George Macready is Dornheimer, and so he plays to his strength as a bad guy after he gets duped. Barbara Nichols is unusually cast as one of the agents. She usually played showgirls or brassy "dames," so it's weird to see her as some kind of super agent. Hugh Beaumont is the head of the NIA! (Now we know what Ward Cleaver's *real* job was!) Richard Arlen of Island of Lost Souls fame has a small role as well.

The special effects aren't very special for a sci-fi movie, and the film might have looked better when screened in a theater. It loses a lot on TV. Those "duplicate" prints, you know, just aren't as good.

THE WALKING DEAD

This Warner Brothers film made it through the so-called horror ban of the latter part of the 1930s. A gangster/horror hybrid, it boasts one of Karloff's best performances.

Karloff plays John Ellman, a patsy for a gang that sets him up to be framed for murder. He's innocent, but he gets the chair anyway because we wouldn't have a movie if he didn't. Edmund Gwenn, (yes, Kris Kringle), is a not-so-mad scientist who believes he can restore Ellman to life. As Dr. Beaumont, he wants the revived Ellman to give him the lowdown on the "other side."

The reanimated Ellman sports a white streak through his hair, has a crippled arm, and a scarred face. Now you would think in any other movie, Ellman would seek out the creeps who framed him and knock them off, but you would be wrong. In an unusual plot twist, Ellman's instincts tell him who was behind the plot and he seeks them out. He just wants to ask them why they had him killed. Every time he finds one of them, they get into a panic from seeing a walking corpse, which causes them to die from a freak accident.

Ellman is shot before the last two of the bad guys get creamed in a car crash. Beaumont is there at the scene to get Ellman to spill the beans about the afterlife before he dies again. But Ellman dies without revealing anything.

In spite of Karloff's scary appearance, he always engenders pity as Ellman. The odd way that the killers meet their death by the hand of fate rather than Ellman gives the film a mystical touch. Maybe Ellman is doling out karma to the bad guys without knowing it.

Warner Brothers' style of fast action and slick production values gave Karloff a nice respite from playing evil monsters, and he gives the role the respect it deserves. Well worth seeing this film if you can track it down.

THE MAD GHOUL

George Zucco ran neck in neck with Lionel Atwill in the mad scientist race. Both had gleaming eyeballs and their reasons for their experiments were either pointless or just plain nuts.

Zucco plays Dr. Morris, who has stumbled upon a formula developed by the Mayans. It's a gas that when breathed in, turns a person into a pliant zombie. Morris has the hots for his lab assistant's girlfriend, Isabel. She is a professional singer who tours with her pianist, Eric. Ted, the lab assistant, knows nothing of this, but Morris deludes himself into thinking that Isabel would much prefer him over Ted. Morris uses the gas on Ted to see if it works and presto, Ted becomes a withered face ghoul. The antidote for Ted's ghoul condition can't be found at the local CVS. The antidote is a serum made from a human heart, living or dead. Morris and Ted become ghoul-friends, as they have to rob graves to get Ted back to normal. Luckily, Ted doesn't remember anything of their late night escapades.

When Morris has a chat with Isabel, he learns that her feelings are for her accompanist, Eric, not for bald, middle-aged nutcases. Morris, who must have a lot of time on his hands, follows Isabel with Ted, as she tours with her concerts. A smart reporter, McClure, sees a pattern that emerges wherever Isabel goes on her tour. Graves get rifled and the hearts are cut out of the corpses. McClure lays a trap in a funeral home for the deadly duo but ends up donating his heart to the cause.

Morris is tired of playing "catch the singer," so he uses his ghoul gas again on Ted, ordering him to kill Eric, then himself. Ted had earlier figured out Morris's nutty plan to get Isabel for himself, and he exposes Morris to the gas before going out for his last errand. The crowd at Isabel's recital gets something not listed on the program when Ted crashes the concert and walks onstage. Police are on the scene already and shoot Ted. At the end we see Morris frantically digging at a grave to get his heart's desire.

The Mad Ghoul is usually dismissed as a lame entry in the Universal B-movie line, but I disagree. First off, the ghoul, played by David Bruce, looks great in Jack Pierce's makeup, which resembles Ardith Bey's face in The Mummy. Bruce is a believable and naive student, and his ignorance of what Morris has done to him, gives him audience sympathy. His monotone ghoul persona is chilling by contrast.

Zucco gets to show his human side when Isabel shatters his illusion. His sad disappointment is somewhat touching.

Evelyn Ankers and Turhan Bey are basically window dressing, but somebody has to be in danger, right?

It's fun to see good old Robert Armstrong as McClure, delivering his lines in the same snappy fashion that Carl Denham would have. It's kind of sad to see him get killed so quickly because his two scenes liven up the film.

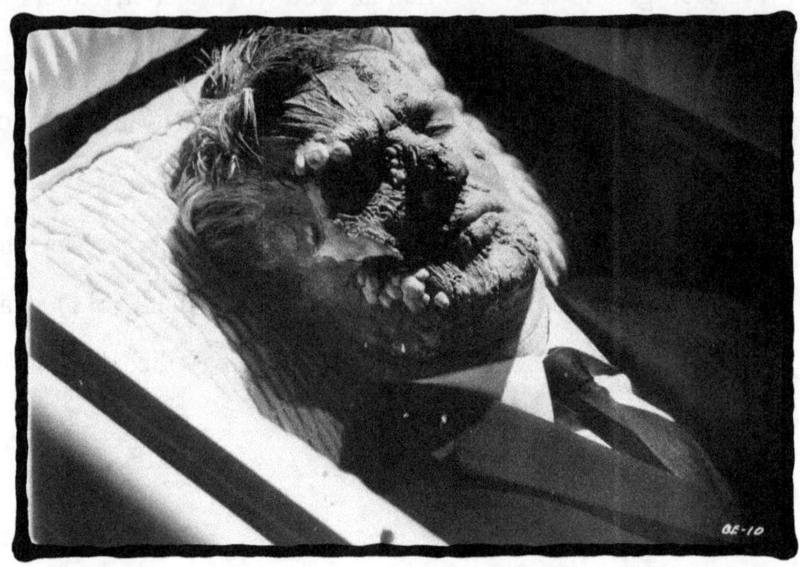

Ever have a vague memory of a movie you saw one Saturday afternoon but don't know the name of? This is one of them. I saw this years ago on a Creature Feature program and pretty much forgot about it. Sometime later the image of the guy pictured above re-entered my brain. I finally tracked it down and saw it again.

I had practically no memory of it, maybe because it isn't very memorable. The cast had familiar faces though: Scott Brady, Hugh Marlowe, Virginia Mayo, and Lisa Gaye.

The film was shot in color, and in the only print I've seen the color is saturated. It's basically an old dark house movie, with beneficiaries of a will being knocked off, or close to it anyway.

The plot centers around a guy named Kovic, who apparently didn't know how to make friends and influence people. The group gathered for a reading of the will all hated his guts. Kovic got his face mashed in a lab accident. His mysterious housekeeper reads the will in which the dead man accuses one of the beneficiaries of knocking him off. How they did this at a long distance, I don't know. We are shown Kovic's body in the coffin, ruined face and all, but we've already seen what appears to be Kovic in his lab. I'm not going to try to explain all the plot machinations, especially since the film is mostly talk and arguments. After a while, you wish Kovic would have knocked more people off his list. As it turns out, it's a robot Kovic that is doing the killing and by the end of the movie, he's out of control and doesn't care who he goes after. The Robo-Kovic doesn't move like a robot. He strolls through the castle as easily as you please. A lot of time is spent watching him traipse through the joint. I couldn't help but think of the robot agent, Hymie in the series Get Smart.

Scott Brady is the hero type in the story, a role he would frequently fall into for cheapo movies like these. His abrasive personality always kind of turned me off, but that's just me.

Lisa Gaye as the love interest has little to do except scream when necessary. She had the lead in a Spanish horror flick titled Face of Terror. She got to be her version of Kovic in that one, as a woman whose badly scarred face is restored by a nice old scientist, played by Fernando Rey. Hugh Marlowe is known for his genre pictures such as World Without End, Earth vs the Flying Saucers and the classic, Day the Earth Stood Still.

WHO IS THAT?

Milton Parsons   If anyone was born to play an undertaker it's this guy. With his bald pate, moon-sized eyes, and long face, he looked like a talking skeleton. I don't know how many times he played a mortician, but he did other types of roles. He was a comical character in The Monster that Challenged the World. He was a homicidal lunatic in The Hidden Hand. He appeared often on TV shows, usually as a take-off of his undertaker character.

Nan Grey This beautiful blonde caught my fancy the first time I saw her as the innocent victim in Dracula's Daughter. She starred opposite Vincent Price in The Invisible Man Returns and showed up in lots of Universal B movies such as The Black Doll and Danger on the Air. Her final appearance was on an episode of the TV series Rawhide.

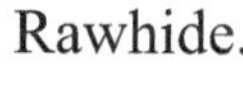

Elisha Cook Known as "Cookie" to his fellow thespians, his kisser is one of the most recognizable faces in the history of cinema. It was always a safe bet that when you saw him, he'd die before the movie was over. He did survive as Wilmer, his most celebrated role, in The Maltese Falcon. He was an innocent man accused of murder in the seminal film noir thriller, Stranger on the Third Floor. He worked well into his senior years, popping up in TV series like Simon and Simon, The Fall Guy, and Alf. He appeared in the movie version of The Night Stalker, and he lived through it! My fave is his role in House on Haunted Hill, when he uttered the famous line, "What's the use of saying good night?"

David Bruce Best known to us monster kids as The Mad Ghoul, Bruce did appear in other thrillers of interest: Inner Sanctum's Calling Dr. Death, The Body Disappears, and The Smiling Ghost. He showed up in small roles in movies but seemed to be most at home on various TV series such as The Lone Ranger, Adventures of Wild Bill Hickcock, The Millionaire, and others. A bit of trivia: he is the uncredited radio announcer's voice in The Mummy's Ghost, in which he speaks of the Mad Doctor of Market Street!

Henry Daniel   If Satan came to Earth in human form he'd look like Henry Daniell. As a matter of fact, he posed as just that entity for a print ad for Bacardi rum. He usually played the heavy and was notable as one of the many actors to play Moriarty in The Woman in Green. His best role for me was as Toddy McFarland in The Body Snatcher, giving his co-star Boris Karloff a run for his money. He appeared on TV frequently as well, in a particularly memorable Thriller episode, Well of Doom.

Billy Bevin Although recognizable as a character actor throughout the sound era, Bevan was a silent comedy star who worked for Mack Sennett. In ten years he made many one and two reel shorts. When sound came in he became a bit or a supporting player in all types of genres. Of note to us, he met Dracula's Daughter and is responsible for reviving Armand Tesla in Return of the Vampire. Many times he was uncredited, but he kept working until the 1950s.

Matt Willis He will always be "Andreas" to us monster kids. His most famous role is in Return of the Vampire, but he had a significant role in the B movie programmer, The Mysterious Doctor. He had numerous uncredited roles, and you can make a game of trying to spot him in the crowd. He appeared in a Shemp Howard Short, Mr. Noisy. Amusing trivia courtesy of the folks at Forgotten Horrors. What does Matt Willis have to do with the Monkees? Mickey Dolenz's mother, Janelle Scott and Matt Willis wrote the song, Pillow Time, which appears on the LP The Monkees Present.

Dennis Hoey Yes, it's Inspector Lestrade, but Hoey had a long career in movies in both England and America. He appeared with Lugosi in an early Hammer film, The Mystery of the Marie Celeste. Although he had many varied roles throughout his career right into the 1950s, he'll always be Lestrade to Holmes fans. He might as well have been Lestrade as the policeman in Frankenstein Meets the Wolf Man. He had on the same getup and acted just like him. It would have been fun if he really was Lestrade. After hearing that Larry Talbot got out of his straitjacket with his teeth he could have said, "Even Holmes wouldn't figure this one out!"

John Dierkes Because of his kisser, he was mostly confined to sinister roles, although he was one of the scientists in The Thing. He was in the genre films, Daughter of Dr. Jekyll and Abbott and Costello meet Dr. Jekyll and Mr. Hyde.

No stranger to Roger Corman, he appeared in The Haunted Palace and The Premature Burial. He also had the distinction of being the nutty preacher who tells Ray Milland to pull out his eyeballs in X: Man with the X-ray eyes.

Michael Mark A familiar face to fans of the Universal classics, he is the grieving father of Maria from the classic, Frankenstein. Usually relegated to small parts, his career spanned the decades and he can be seen in films and TV series right into the late 1960s. For genre fans, he is the scientist who creates the serum in The Wasp Woman.

Gloria Talbot One of the more recognizable genre actors, but like Beverly Garland, you couldn't characterize her as the shrinking violet type. His most memorable role was the heroine in I Married a Monster from Outer Space. She co-starred in the Bert I. Gordon fun flick, The Cyclops. She graced Edgar Ulmer's Daughter of Dr. Jekyll, and she got to play a villainous role in The Leech Woman. Early in her career you can spot her in the Abbott and Costello TV series, Boston Blackie, Cisco Kid, Hopalong

Cassidy, and The Adventures of Superman. I count her among my favorite heroines, along with Beverly Garland and Evelyn Ankers.

Luana Walters   She appeared in numerous movies throughout her career, but unfortunately, many times was uncredited. Her biggest role was the female lead in The Corpse Vanishes, and she had a supporting role in the serial, Shadows Over Chinatown, both times sharing the screen with Bela Lugosi. She had uncredited parts in Mighty Joe Young and the She Creature, and played Lara, Superman's mother, in the first Superman serial with Kirk Alyn.

Louise Curry Another actor that found herself stuck in poverty row studios such as Monogram and PRC. She appeared in Voodoo Man and The Ape Man. She did two serials for Columbia, the classic Captain Marvel, and the Masked Marvel. Out of her many uncredited parts, it's fun to note she was a reporter in Citizen Kane. She gave up on the biz during the 1950s.

Byron Foulger Usually specializing in milquetoast roles, his career spanned from the early 1930s into 1970. His high pitched quavering voice made him the perfect guy to be pushed around. He could show up in almost any movie, big studio or small, and also was all over the tube, usually playing the same type of character. Adept at comedy as well, his most peculiar role was as the unseen voice of the father in the short-lived comedy series, Captain Nice.

Wanda McKay This appealing actor appears in both Monograms and PRC specials such as The Black Raven, The Monster Maker, Voodoo Man, and Bowery at Midnight. Like a lot of B movie alumni, she did a lot of early TV shows like The Lone Ranger and The Cisco Kid.

Charles Halton As a bit and supporting player, this guy was everywhere in a career starting in silent movies into the 1950s. He usually portrayed annoying, priggish characters. He was the nosey neighbor in the B movie classic,

Stranger on the Third Floor, and was also in the genre pictures, Dr. Cyclops, Man with Nine Lives, and The Body Disappears. Like everyone else on the planet, he appeared in The Lone Ranger TV show. He might be one of the few actors who *didn't* appear in The Cisco Kid.

John McGuire Mostly confined to uncredited bit roles, McGuire's best role was in the noir classic, Stranger on the Third Floor, so he shared the screen with two other of our B movie friends, Charles Halton and Elisha Cook. He played the twin brothers in The Invisible Ghost, one of the better Lugosi Monograms.

Wallace Ford This guy has the distinction of appearing in two of the weirdest movies ever made: The Ape Man and Freaks. A capable supporting actor in both A and B pictures, Ford is most known to us monster kids for slumming in Poverty Row studios such as Monogram. What a list of B's he was in! Night of Terror, One Frightened Night, Rogue's Tavern, Murder by Invitation, and the egregiously racist, Mysterious Mr. Wong. Of course, he was in the first Kharis movie, The Mummy's Hand, and then got bumped off in The Mummy's Tomb, which I always thought was a shame.

Dick Miller Talk about a cult actor. One of Roger Corman's mainstays, you can see him doing bit parts as in Not of this Earth, or a star in Bucket of Blood or War of the Satellites. He turned down the role of Seymour in Little Shop of Horrors because he felt it was too close to the character he just played in Bucket of Blood. His pal, Jonathan Haze got the part that made him immortal to B movie fans. Miller and Haze had cameos in X: The Man with the X-Ray Eyes as two hecklers in an audience. Miller had a long career in movies and TV and you can spot him in later films like The Howling and Gremlins.

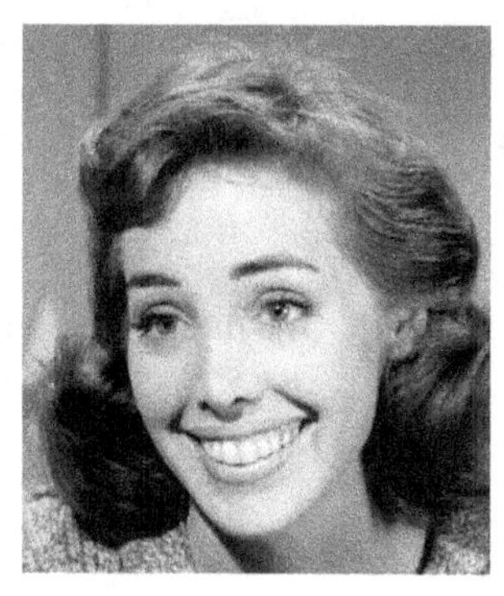

Barboura Morris I never saw Barbara spelled that way before, but when I saw this Barboura, I was in love. Her all too short career in B-movies was cut short when she succumbed to cancer just after her 43rd birthday. Her prominent roles were in Bucket of Blood, Wasp Woman, and Machine Gun Kelly, where she was kidnapped by rising star, Charles Bronson. Another actress who worked uncredited, you can spot her in The Haunted Palace, The

Dunwich Horror, The Trip, The Wild Angels, and Teenage Caveman.

Jonathan Haze Haze appeared in Roger Corman's first movie, The Monster from the Ocean Floor. He will always be remembered for playing Seymour in Little Shop of Horrors. He had supporting roles in Not of this Earth, It Conquered the World, and The Terror. I spotted him once on the TV series 77 Sunset Strip.

Hillary Brooke Hillary had to be a good sport to put up with Abbott and Costello in their TV series. Adept at playing a villainess, she was Moriarty's partner in The Woman in Green, but could also be the put upon heroine in the Holmes movie, Sherlock Holmes Faces Death. She was at her scariest in Invaders from Mars, once the evil Martians had put a chip in her neck to make her the nasty mother of the year.

Cecil Kellaway was one of the most adorable character actors of the day. Usually, his characters were affable, but he played a clever policeman in The Invisible Man Returns. He also was in the first

Kharis mummy movie, The Mummy's Hand. He appeared frequently on television in genre shows such as The Twilight Zone.

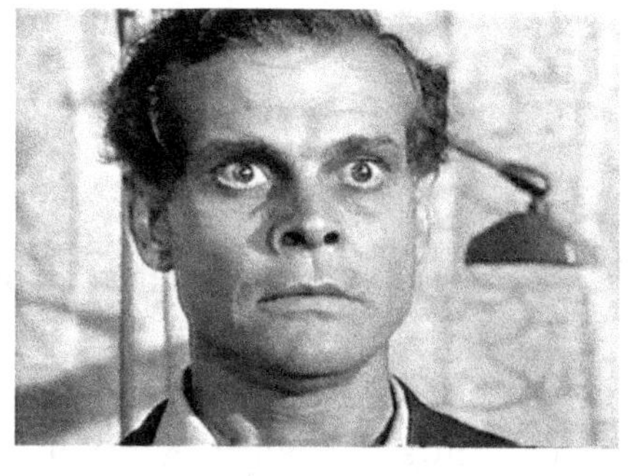

Glenn Dixon The only reason I have him here is that he scared the hell out of me in Voodoo Island. I was around 5 years old at the time, but he haunted my nightmares for a while.

Dabbs Greer was one of the most ubiquitous character actors in film and TV. He was in the horror gem, The Vampire with John Beal. He was all over the place on the boob tube: Adventures of Superman, Perry Mason, Twilight Zone, Outer Limits, Science Fiction Theater; you name it, he was in it.

Douglas Dumbrille was usually cast as a sleazeball. One look at him and you couldn't trust him. He was in the genre films The Frozen Ghost, The Cat Creeps, and The Catman of Paris. He was also a good foil for the comedians Abbott and Costello and The Marx Brothers.

Eduardo Ciannelli got the Kharis mummy series off to a good start by inaugurating George Zucco as the first high priest to *not* fulfill his mission due to his uncontrollable lust. He was great in the serial The Mysterious Dr. Satan. His robot henchman was one of those lovable box-like automatons. Another fixture on TV, you can spot him on Thriller, Man from U.N.C.L.E, and The Time Tunnel.

Herb Vigran was the epitome of a working actor. Small roles, supporting roles, walk-ons; he did them all. His distinctive voice and face made him easy to spot no matter the decade. He was frequently on The Adventures of Superman TV series, almost always as a criminal. He showed up a lot on Gunsmoke as Judge Brooker. I think if you sat in front of the TV all day watching a nostalgia station like MeTV, you'd see him somewhere every hour.

Paul Cavanaugh had a long career in movies and TV. His genre credits include The Strange Case of Doctor Rx, two films in the Holmes series, (Women in Green, House of Fear), House of Wax, Bride of the Gorilla, The Man Who Turned to Stone and became a shrunken head in Four Skulls of Jonathan Drake.

Skelton Knaggs Here's another actor that has the face you can't forget. His pockmarked kisser usual pegged him as a bad guy, such as in the Holmes movie, Terror By Night, Dick Tracy meets Gruesome and House of Dracula. He did get to play good guys though. He was the deaf mute in Val Lewton's Ghost Ship, and a servant to Anna Lee in Bedlam. But his face was his fortune, and with his silky British accent, he was always memorable, if uncredited.

I'm sure most of these actors would be wondering why we would care who they are. For them, they were just doing a job like anyone else, and besides, they weren't big stars like Gable, Bogart, or Garbo. But as many big stars flare up and burn out just as quickly, these character actors left an indelible impression on every film in which they appeared. They were like old friends who would drop by for a brief visit but would most assuredly return in a little while. If I had been a professional actor in the movies, I would want to be another Herb Vigran. Any job, any size. If the movie is a flop, you can't blame me. As long as I'm working, I'd be happy.

ENDLESS HALLOWEEN

To sum it all up, we monster kids are addicted to these films. We love all kinds; from the classics to the most threadbare of B-movies.

I look forward to Halloween every year. Not for handing out candy. I never get any kids coming to the door anymore, which is a damn shame. I still buy a bag or two, just in case. Strangely enough, I end up eating it all myself.

No, Halloween, is somewhat like Christmas to us. Both holidays tend to make you feel nostalgic for when you were a kid, but unlike Christmas, for us oldsters who have lost most of their family to the passing of time, Halloween is the holiday when we can commune with those who never die; Dracula, Frankenstein, The Wolf Man, The Mummy, the Creature from the Black Lagoon, Gort, Robot Monster, Audrey Junior, Dr.

Jekyll and Mr. Hyde, and a slew of others. We can see our friends when we pop the DVD in the player or if we stream it, if so inclined. They are the only friends we grew up with that never leave us. And so, as Tiny Tim observed, "God bless them, everyone!"

Michael Legge is an independent film maker operating under the name of Sideshow Cinema. His feature films include **Working Stiffs, Loons, My Mouth Lies Screaming, Crawlers, Coffee Run** and **Evan Straw,** among others. These

movies can found for sale at his Sideshow Cinema website. They can also be seen via numerous streaming services.

As horror host Dr. Dreck, along with Moaner, (Lorna Nogueira), he has headed the cable program, Dungeon of Dr. Dreck, featuring public domain horror, science fiction and mysteries. The program is available nationwide via local stations, and online at Betamax TV and the Eerie Late Night Horror Channel. He has written three books; **Dr. Dreck's B Movie Museum, Monster Kidding, Outlandish Adventures, Lurking in the Late Night, and the Reddy Boys mysteries, Deader than Dead and The Deserted Drive-In.**

www.ingramcontent.com/pod-product-compliance
Lightning Source LLC
Chambersburg PA
CBHW051959150726

47999CB00004B/1452